D0948058

THE UNOFFICIAL HUNGER GAMES

WILDERNESS SURVIVAL GUIDE

CREEK STEWART

LIVING READY BOOKS
IOLA, WISCONSIN
www.LivingReadyOnline.com

CONTENTS

INTRODUCTION

LET THE GAMES BEGIN

I've been an avid outdoorsman all my life, and that interest has led me down a unique path to a very interesting job. I am a survival instructor and own a survival and preparedness training facility called Willow Haven Outdoor. I teach survival skills for a living. It's certainly not your average nine-to-five job and "wilderness survival" wasn't on the list of majors to choose from when I went to college. Nonetheless, this is where I ended up and I *love* what I do.

I remember when a friend first told me about The Hunger Games book series. With all of the survival skills mentioned, he thought it would be right up my alley. He was right! I really enjoyed all three books—especially the constant mention of different survival skills, tactics and strategies. However, with the mention of each survival skill, I found myself "hungry" for more. Just the mention of these skills wasn't enough to satisfy me. I needed details! When Katniss gathers edible roots, I wanted to know which plants! When she set twitch-up snares, I wanted to know exactly what kind of snares! When Peeta camouflaged himself, I wanted to know how he did it! When Rue chewed up plants to make a medicine for tracker jacker stings, I wanted details then, too! Were these real survival skills?

Could they be used if you or I were in a real-life survival situation? If so, how can we learn them? Well, it's your lucky day. Why? Because, like I said, this is what I do for a living—I teach survival skills. If *The Hunger Games* left you hungry for more survival details, too, then this book is for you. Whether you love *The Hunger Games* or just love survival, look at this book as an extension of the skills used by Katniss, her friends, and her enemies to stay alive in desperate situations. This is your *Unofficial Hunger Games Wilderness Survival Guide*.

Let me start by saying, yes, many of the survival skills and strategies mentioned in The Hunger Games book series are based on real survival skills. In this book, I have categorized and compiled these skills along with the details and step-by-step instructions you need to practice these skills in real life. I've also included many other survival skills that I imagine the characters in the book series would use behind the scenes to stay alive. These are time-tested and field-tested survival skills that can save your life.

AND THIS YEAR'S TRIBUTE FOR THE GAMES IS

_____!

(Write your name here)

Sometimes it happens like that—out of the blue, without warning. Our names can be drawn from life's big, round reaping jar at any given moment. We don't live in Panem and the disasters we face are not called the Hunger Games, but we are still at risk of being thrust into a survival situation every day of our lives. And, unfortunately, this risk does not stop when we turn eighteen.

WHY STUDY SURVIVAL SKILLS?

Besides being fun, learning survival skills is very practical. Bad things happen to good people. Sometimes, a plane crashes and strands passengers for a few days. Cars break down on deserted roads and leave people to fend for themselves until help arrives. Hikers get lost in the woods. Natural disasters like floods, earthquakes, and tornados strike all the time and turn life upside down for a while. All kinds of survival situations occur to regular people on a regular basis. It's just the reality of living in an imperfect world. You may very well find yourself (alone or with others) in a real-life survival scenario one day. Many people who attend my survival training courses do so because they have a family. Do you love and care for anyone? Do they know life-saving survival skills?

EXPECT THE UNEXPECTED

Never make the mistake of assuming that everything will always be perfect.

The world we live in, like Panem, is becoming increasingly unstable. One undisputable fact about history is that it does not lie. We can learn from what has already happened and plan for the future. Once the future happens, it's history. You can't control the future but you can control how equipped you are to deal with whatever may happen in your life from this point forward. The future does not "surprise" a student of survival. Survival skills prepare us for the "what ifs" in life. What if things don't go as planned? What if you have to build a fire? Or make a survival shelter? Or hunt for your own food? Survivors prepare now for the unexpected events that may happen in the future.

IF IT'S WORTH HAVING, IT'S WORTH THE EFFORT

Anything that's worth having in life requires effort. Survival skills are no exception. I wish I could promise that you'll be an expert survivalist as soon as you finish reading this book. I can't. Katniss spent many, many hours in the woods perfecting her survival skills and, like her, you will need to practice as well. If you are serious about really learning Katniss's survival skills, then you will have to practice—period. The good news is that you don't have to be deep in the woods of District 12 to practice.

Almost every skill detailed in this book can be perfected right in your backyard. There is a big misconception that you have to be alone in the wilderness or on a deserted island to practice survival skills. You don't! Your back yard is your arena!

WHERE'S MY SILVER PARACHUTE?

Unfortunately, many people don't prepare for the "what ifs" in life. They don't take the time to learn survival skills that could one day bridge that razor-thin gap between life and death. Sometimes I really think they believe a silver parachute might float down and provide them with exactly what they need when they need it. Maybe it's that they expect a magical tip from their sponsor. You and I both know this doesn't happen anywhere but in Panem. And the last time I checked, I couldn't find Panem on my map, though I was never really that good with geography. When the parachute doesn't come or the survival tip doesn't sound out through the loud speaker in the sky, what will they do?

ARE THE ODDS IN YOUR FAVOR?

I'll admit, I can't stand the Career Tributes. They are cocky, well fed, well trained, and blood-thirsty. Even though I don't like them, I can't argue with the fact they have better odds of surviving the Hunger Games. Why? Simple—they are better prepared. They have entered into a survival situation with practice, training, and a preparedness mentality. They prepare for the games *before* their names are chosen at the reaping. They know this is the key to increasing the odds of survival. Once your name is drawn, it's too late. If you haven't prepared in advance, the odds *are not* in your favor. Survival mentality is the first and most important survival skill.

TO SURVIVE, YOU NEED TO PREPARE AND THINK LIKE A VICTOR.

ONE

SURVIVAL MENTALITY: THINK LIKE A VICTOR

SO, YOUR NAME HAS BEEN PULLED from life's reaping jar. Tributes have time to train and prepare before they enter the arena and face the ultimate survival situation. In the real world, you never know when Mother Nature will pull your name from the jar and thrust you into a life-or-death survival situation. Think I'm being overly dramatic? Turn on the evening news and count how many stories relate to natural disasters—wildfires, earthquakes, floods, tornadoes, hurricanes. Real people are affected by these situations every day and often there is little to no warning. You have to prepare in advance.

The first chapter in every survival book should be about *attitude*. Your survival mentality will have a huge impact on the outcome of the situation. Attitude is the rudder that steers your ship. It can keep you on a focused and deliberate course of action, or it can send you crashing into the rocks. Though invisible, your mentality is the most powerful force behind getting out of a nasty situation alive. It can also be your worst enemy. If you choose to give up and feel like a victim, you are signing your own death sentence. When you give up mentally, the rest of your body follows suit.

VICTORS HAVE GOALS

Whether she's gathering food beyond the fence or surviving the arena, Katniss is driven by clear and concise goals.

The first step in any survival situation is to set goals. In a survival situation, aimless wandering is a waste of valuable time and energy. Many people panic when thrust into a survival scenario. Panic leads to poor, and potentially fatal, decisions. Goals help reduce panic by giving you clarity, pushing you forward, and helping you focus on specific tasks. Some sample survival goals are:

- I must build a shelter by dusk tonight.
- I must start a fire.
- If help has not arrived in three days, I will head east toward the river.
- I will set four snares before I going to sleep tonight.
- I will build a signal fire as soon as the sun comes up in the morning.

Victors set goals and pursue them relentlessly. Instead of just "going with the flow" of life, victors strive with purpose to achieve meaningful goals. How can you expect to go anywhere if you haven't first chosen a destination?

VICTORS ARE BRAVE

Bravery is a prerequisite to victory. Cowards are only successful at failure. If I could describe Katniss in one word, it would be *brave*. Brave people are not fearless. They simply decide to stare fear in the face and press on anyway. Bravery is not the absence of fear, but rather the ability to overcome fear and persevere through it. Katniss displays unparalleled bravery time and time again when the odds are definitely not in her favor. The word *impossible* is not in her vocabulary and failure is not an acceptable outcome. Katniss knows that without risk there is no reward.

Victors are not only brave for themselves, but for others as well. No one follows a cowardly leader. Even after volunteering for the Hunger Games, Katniss is brave for her mother and Prim. And, in those same moments, Gale has to be brave for Katniss. Surround yourself with brave people. Sometimes, you must *decide* to be brave even when everything in you wants to be scared. Katniss leads a nation to revolt not because she wasn't scared but because she didn't let fear prevent her from acting on her convictions.

VICTORS ARE POSITIVE THINKERS

Sun Tzu, an ancient Chinese military general, once said "Victorious warriors win first and then go to war, while defeated warriors go to war first and then seek to win."

Everyone has moments of self-doubt. It's natural to question yourself. Every survival battle begins in the mind. You must first win over your mind before you can expect to conquer any circumstance. Survival is 90 percent mental and 10 percent physical. Katniss never lets self-doubt get the best of her. She stays positive and therefore stays alive!

Victors understand that attitude determines destiny. It has been said that whether you think you can or you think you can't, you're right either way. Negative expectations will always produce negative results. Survival scenarios present many hurdles. Katniss repeatedly faces overwhelming odds but never focuses on the problem. She focuses on the solution. She transforms impossible circumstances with "possible" thinking.

VICTORS DON'T GIVE UP

I have a deep respect for Katniss. That girl is a fighter. She *never* gives up. Even after being burned, knocked out, blown down, trapped in a tree, cut, shot, broken, dehydrated, medicated, starved, deafened and mentally tortured, she still never gives up. Her will to survive often overcomes the seemingly unmanageable situations she finds herself in. Even Peeta maintains a positive attitude when he is left for dead. He greets Katniss with a smile and a positive attitude when she finds him in serious trouble in the arena. Not only do they not give up on themselves, Katniss and Peeta never give up on each other. Victors don't give up on their friends, either.

VICTORS FORM ALLIANCES

Working together is a prevalent theme throughout all three books in the The Hunger Games trilogy. Developing partnerships and alliances lets you share resources and skill sets with fellow survivors. Katniss and Gale learn this early on. Life in District 12 is a daily survival situation in itself. In exchange for a bow, Gale teaches Katniss trapping skills and together they are an incredibly successful hunting team. When one is sick or absent, the other can still provide fresh game to trade.

Katniss continues this survival strategy inside the arena by forming alliances with Rue and Peeta. Here, we realize that an alliance can mean more than just sharing survival resources and knowledge. Companionship and friendship are intrinsic human needs and make any survival scenario more bearable. True, meaningful relationships can develop from survival alliances. After all, it is the re-

lationship between Katniss and other tributes that united an entire nation.

Everyone has a skill. Some peoples' skills may be more obvious than others, but it's important to find the value that each person can offer in a survival scenario. It must be a *win-win* relationship. Everyone has different backgrounds and life experiences that can be beneficial. This is illustrated perfectly throughout the Quarter Quell as Katniss and her allies depend on each other's unique skills from their respective districts: Beetee's engineering knowledge, Finnick's fishing and ocean-related skills and Katniss's well-rounded survival abilities. Again, in book three, as Katniss's small squadron makes its way through the capitol's labyrinth of streets and tunnels, teamwork proves crucial to surviving and accomplishing a common goal. From keeping watch while others slept to defending from enemy fire, working with others was the only way to survive.

There is power in numbers. If at all possible, use teamwork to meet survival goals. Partnering with other can have exponential survival payoffs.

VICTORS ADAPT AND IMPROVISE

There is a reason why the United States Marine Corps have popularized the motto "Improvise, adapt, and overcome." They are keenly aware that the ability to adapt and improvise is absolutely necessary to success. If you cannot or do not improvise, your chances of survival are slim to none. Improvising is more of a mental skill than a physical skill. It is the ability to think creatively and use the resources you've been given to meet your basic survival needs. If you had everything you needed to survive, you wouldn't be in a survival situation. It's the lack of what you need that makes things dangerous. Using *what you have to get what you need* is the key.

Many items can be creatively used for multiple purposes. For example, the 3' (1m) square of plastic that Katniss grabbed at the start of her first Hunger Games can be used in countless ways to meet survival goals, including shelter, solar still, water collection, poncho, ground cloth, and container. Many of these uses are discussed in the following chapters.

For some, thinking outside the box when it comes to meeting survival goals can be a challenge. Begin by looking at an everyday item and list three ways it can be used directly or indirectly to meet one of your basic survival needs: shelter, water, fire, or food. You may even surprise yourself.

VICTORS PREPARE IN ADVANCE

Victors try to eliminate risk by preparing for the unexpected. Katniss continually hones her hunting and survival skills to provide for Prim and her mom in District 12. This practice and preparation pays off when she enters the arena and has to rely on her skills to survive. She is also able to provide for Peeta, who is much less practiced in survival skills.

The Career Tributes prepare for the Hunger Games years in advance and therefore have better odds of surviving. The same is true in our life. If we take time now to learn survival skills that we might need later, the odds begin to shift in our favor. There still are no guarantees, but it does increase our chances. I grew up in Boy Scouts, and they say it best with their no-nonsense survival motto: "Be prepared."

VICTORS LIVE FOR WHAT THEY LOVE

The human spirit is strongest when it's fighting for something or someone else. Katniss fights for Prim. Peeta fights for Katniss. Gale fights for freedom. None of them fight for themselves. There is something powerful about fighting for something greater than yourself. Survivors know *why* they want to live. The greatest survival stories of all time are motivated not by the fear of dying, but the fear of losing what makes life worth living. For some, that is a cause; for many, that is a person or family. Search your soul and find that one thing other than yourself that makes surviving your only option. The flame will burn for this long after the one for yourself has gone out.

SUMMARY

Attitude is important, but sometimes the will to live just isn't enough. You need preparedness and skill to step in to pick up the slack. This is where the fun begins.

When I teach survival skills, I always start with what I call the Core Four. These are the four most basic human survival needs that have been the same since the beginning of time.

Your Core Four Basic Human Survival Needs are:

- Shelter
- Water
- Fire
- Food

These four needs are loosely based on the Three Survival Rules of Three:

In extreme conditions…

1. You can live for three hours without shelter.
2. You can live for three days without water.
3. You can live for three weeks without food.

Katniss and many of the other characters throughout The Hunger Games trilogy are constantly trying to secure one or more of these Core Four needs with a variety of survival skills and strategies. Survival is a way of life for the citizens of Panem, whether they are competing in the games or surviving life in the districts.

In the following chapters I will detail many of the skills you can use in the arena and in real-life survival situations. I start with the Core Four for a reason. If you are ever in a survival situation, these are the four areas that typically need to be addressed first to keep you alive!

TWO

SURVIVAL SHELTER: MOTHER NATURE IS THE ULTIMATE GAMEMAKER

THERE IS NOTHING that Seneca Crane or any of the Capitol's Gamemakers could conjure up to compete with what Mother Nature has already unleashed on this earth. Make no bones about it, Mother Nature is in control, period. She makes the rules. She claims more lives each year than I'd care to imagine. She can make the cannon with your name on it sound off faster than almost any other threat on the planet.

What is Mother Nature's most deadly weapon? Hypothermia. Hypothermia is when your core body temperature drops dangerously low. More people die of hypothermia each year than any other outdoor-related injury or accident. Hypothermia is the no. 1 outdoor killer. Our best defense from hypothermia is shelter. Remember the first of the Survival Rules of Three: In extreme conditions, you can live for three hours without shelter. Three hours— that's how fast hypothermia can take you out.

FIRE BALLS, TIDAL WAVES, FLESH-EATING INSECTS, OH MY...

Seeking, finding, and making shelter is a big deal in the arena. Tributes use shelter for many purposes. Some include:

- protection from the Gamemakers
- protection from other tributes
- protection from predators
- protection from exposure to weather elements—heat, cold, rain, snow

Katniss takes cover in a variety of makeshift shelters. Some of them include:

Cliff ledge protected

Poison ivy on forest floor

Ant mound

- A tree
- A cave
- A debris nest: a pile of leaves and pine needles on a cold night in the arena
- A woven grass hut

During her first Hunger Games, Katniss also has a heat-reflective sleeping bag and a 3' (1m) square piece of plastic. She uses both of those items to protect herself from the elements. We will touch on these a bit later. But first, let's go over survival sheltering basics.

CHOOSING YOUR SHELTER

In a survival situation, there are five elements to consider when choosing your shelter location and design. Planning is paramount. Here's some valuable advice I learned early in my survival-skills career: *don't rush.* Rushing leads to foolish mistakes that

you will most certainly regret later. A rookie mistake in the shelter department could easily cost you your life, and that's a fact many people have learned throughout history. Below are the five elements to consider before you choose a shelter site or design.

1. Location Consideration: Dry

No matter what kind of weather, region, or environment you find yourself in, you must choose the driest possible shelter site. Wet and/or moist shelters kill people. If you are wet, you can develop hypothermia in temperatures as high as 50°F (10°C).

Remember, water travels downhill so, typically, elevated areas are drier. Southward-facing site locations are also drier because they receive sunlight as the sun travels east to west. Areas protected by cliffs, ledges, or tree canopies tend to be drier as well because they are protected from rain.

Avoid depressions, valleys, and low spots. Never camp close to running water, streams, rivers, or canyon valleys. Flash floods from areas upstream can raise water levels for miles downstream with little to no warning. Just a few years ago, several campers in Arkansas were killed when their campsite was suddenly overtaken by floodwaters.

2. Location Consideration: Survey for Natural Hazards

Flash flood areas mentioned above are prime examples of naturally hazardous areas. Other well-known hazards include:

- **Poisonous Plants:** An allergic reaction to a plant, such as poison ivy, can be a devastating first aid emergency to someone in a survival situation. A quick survey of the shelter location and a basic knowledge of poisonous plants can prevent this.

- **Stinging or Biting Insects:** Learn from the group sleeping under Katniss when she dropped that tracker jacker nest on them. Though tracker jackers aren't real, we have plenty of stinging and biting insects that can make your life pretty miserable. Biting ants, tarantulas, scorpions, and yellow jackets are all ground-dwelling critters that, in certain circumstances, can be downright deadly. The best rule of thumb is to thoroughly check the ground *before*

Rock cliff with fallen rocks

Widowmaker branches

making camp. Scrape away leaves and debris and make sure the ground is free of nests, holes, or mounds. Then, simply pile the debris back on.

- **Rock cliffs:** Falling rocks can be deadly. A good policy is to inspect the ground around any cliff you are considering. If it's littered with rocks, then it probably means rocks fall from that cliff. If there aren't any fallen rocks, then it's a safe bet.
- **Widowmakers:** Big, dead limbs in trees are called widowmakers for a reason. You can be injured or killed by even a small limb if it falls from high up in a tree. Inspect any trees that you are considering sleeping under. If it has some dead limbs and branches, don't risk it. High winds can send those crashing down on your shelter in the middle of the night.

3. Location Consideration: Shelter Near Resources

You need some resources to meet your basic survival needs. Katniss knows this and often chooses a shelter area near water. Below is a list of resources to consider when choosing your shelter site:

- **Water:** Water is a precious resource and should always, if possible, be a short walk from your camp. Besides hydration, water may be needed for cooking, washing tools, bathing, or washing clothes. Ideally, your camp should be located no farther than 100 yards (91m) (the length of a football field) from a water source to help you conserve as much energy as possible. You won't have to spend energy traveling long distances to access and/or carry water back to camp.
- **Building materials:** If the shelter design you've chosen requires building materials, it's smart to locate your camp near those materials. If you are building a cold-weather debris hut (discussed later), don't choose a campsite far away from dried leaves and trees. It will take a lot of energy to transport shelter-building materials even short distances.
- **Fuel:** It takes an insane amount of firewood to keep a descent fire burning through the night. If you are depending on fire for warmth, try your absolute best to strategically locate your shelter site near the largest amounts of fuel. Again, carrying firewood uses up calories that at some point will need to

be replaced, which can be difficult if food is scarce.

4. Design Consideration: Shelter Purpose

The shelter style you choose should be heavily influenced by *why* you need a shelter. What is the purpose of your shelter? My experience is primarily from the Eastern Woodlands in the United States—a four-season environment with terrain that ranges from swamps and prairies to mountains and dense forests. This environment is also much like the one found in District 12 and the arena design in Katniss's first Hunger Games, so this is the environment we will focus on. In an Eastern Woodland-type of environment, there are three main shelter purposes:

- **Cold Weather Shelter:** Protects primarily from exposure to the cold, including rain.
- **Mild Weather Shelter:** Protects primarily from rain, dew and/ or sun.
- **Elevated Shelter:** Built in lowland swamp areas where ground-level shelters are not an option.

There are no black-and-white rules to shelter configurations. Every scenario is different, which is why it's absolutely critical that you be able to improvise. However, learning some basic shelter configurations for a variety of scenarios will give you a knowledge base to work from. Your creativity and on-hand resources will fill in the blanks. Mother Nature may also be feeling a bit generous, but I'll discuss that in a bit.

5. Design and Location Consideration: Energy Conservation

Energy conservation should be at the forefront of every survival decision you make—especially shelter. Building even a simple survival shelter can be a very labor-intensive task. I've worked eight hours of back-breaking labor building cold-weather debris huts that, in the end, gave me only the bare minimum shelter I needed. Working like this spends thousands

Rock ledge shelter

of calories, and that will eventually catch up with you. I'm not suggesting that you be lazy, but rather make intelligent decisions that help you save time and energy. Try to develop a partnership with Mother Nature instead of working against her. Let her do some work for you if you can. I'll elaborate below.

SURVIVAL SHELTERS USED BY KATNISS AND FRIENDS
The Gimme

There is nothing wrong with using a shelter that Mother Nature has already built for you. It makes energy-saving survival sense. Let her do the work and you save the calories. I call these natural-built shelters a "Gimme." Katniss and Peeta make good use of a Gimme in the arena when they make camp in a cave. It protects them for days from the rain and cold, and they have to do very little work to stay there. It is pretty much "move-in ready," just the way I like shelters to be.

I've seen a variety of Gimme shelters in nature. Some of them include:

- caves and rock ledges
- hollow trees
- under the lower branches of pine boughs in heavy snow fall
- under or beside large fallen trees
- behind the root-ball of fallen trees

Mother Nature may not give you an entire shelter, but often she'll give you at least one wall to work with. As you'll see a little later, a fallen tree or a large rock makes an excellent wall for a lean-to style shelter.

Hollow tree

Pine bough snow shelter

Elevated Shelters: Sleep with the Mockingjays

Katniss prefers sleeping in the trees. While hunting in District 12, the trees are her safe haven away from predators. In the arena, the trees keep her above and away from other tributes. Her knowledge of sleeping in an elevated shelter saves her life on more than one occasion.

In a real-life survival situation, sleeping above the ground is most applicable in extremely wet or swampy areas where building a camp on the ground is not an option. Here are three elevated survival shelter options:

Katniss and Rue's Bare Branch Roost: Primitive jungle cultures that make their homes high in the forest canopy still exist today. One of the many reasons they live in trees is the exposure to a steady wind that keeps biting gnats and mosquitoes away from them as they sleep. I'm sure the view is nice, too.

If you find the right large tree, sleeping on a branch might be an excellent Gimme shelter to keep you off the ground. This is certainly a risky venture, and Katniss has the right idea by using her belt as a safety harness. Roping yourself in is an absolute necessity or shelter will be the least of your problems. A broken back really complicates a survival situation. If you don't have a belt or rope, you can make cordage from bark or other natural resources. See chapter five for instructions.

Not all trees are created equal. Skip the perfect trees because they are typically too difficult to climb. Search for trees with some character. And by character, I mean imperfections, such

Tree root wind block shelter

Sleeping on a sycamore branch

as knots and burls. Trees with past wounds from long-ago storms also make perfect roosting spots. These features can be nature's ladder to a low-hanging branch or nook.

Burl ladder on monster white oak

Three-tree elevated platform

Mature oak trees, large sycamores, and gnarly cypress trees make excellent climbing and sleeping candidates. I've also found that mulberry trees are especially prone to wacky growth patterns and often have accessible, large, low-hanging branches. And if it's the right season, you can gorge yourself on sweet berries before dozing off to sleep.

Platform Shelter: In my opinion, if you want an elevated shelter, a platform shelter is the more practical option than sleeping in a tree. Platform shelters can be set up in a huge variety of ways. You typically need to use some type of cordage, but some platform shelters can be set up without rope if you get creative.

The basic concept is to create a platform above the ground by lashing poles to trees or tripods and then topping these poles with a floor-like platform. Your creativity is the limit. Two elevated shelter options are the three-tree elevated platform and the A-frame elevated platform.

Whenever you build a platform shelter, be sure to test it before you put your own weight on it. Push on it with your arms or place a heavy object on it to make sure it will support your weight. You don't want to fall.

Improvised Hammock Shelters: Hammocks are an age-old option for sleeping off the ground. You can create a makeshift hammock by securing a tarp or canvas diagonally between two trees. Tie cordage to each tree. Find rocks about the size of golf balls and wrap one rock in each corner of the tarp. Then tie the cordage below the rocks. The rocks will serve as anchor points and keep the corners from ripping out.

Primitive tribes have been using native vines and natural cordage for centuries to make hammocks. Using the same A-frame structure in the A-frame elevated platform photo, I quickly wrapped a hammock-style sleeping platform using lengths of inner tree barked that I stripped from a walnut tree that had been struck by lightning. Continuously wrap the bark around the two horizontal poles until it will hold your weight. No knots required!

A-frame elevated platform

Improvised tarp hammock

Debris Huts and Nests: Nature's Blanket

During her time in the arena, Katniss takes shelter under some bushes and creates a small debris nest using leaves and pine needles to keep her warm throughout the night. This is a cold-weather shelter option. Just as people use lightweight, fluffy insulation in their walls and attics to keep out the cold, we can keep cold away from our bodies by covering ourselves with forest debris—leaves,

Inner tree bark hammock A-frame

Makeshift debris nest of dead leaves

grasses, pine needles, cattail down—anything that resembles lightweight insulation material.

Like insulation, piles of dead leaves, grasses, and pine needles create *dead air space*. Dead air is air that is trapped within the debris. A layer of dead air helps keep cold air from reaching you from the outside and keeps your body heat next to your body instead of letting it escape.

Almost every nesting animal I can think of—from squirrels to raccoons—uses this exact same method. Why? Because it works! Debris nests are simple to make. Make a huge pile of leaves and forest debris and crawl inside. Be sure to place some debris under you as well to prevent the cold earth from sucking the warmth out of you.

Remember when I talked about building your shelter near important resources? If you build a debris nest or hut, you'll want to be near lots of leaves, grasses, or pine needles. The great thing is that in cold months, when you need lots of dead leaves, Mother Nature helps you out by dropping them on the ground for you to scoop up.

Debris Hut: A debris hut is a more organized and elaborate version of a debris nest. It involves building a

 YOUR SPONSOR HAS SENT YOU A

SURVIVAL QUICK TIP

Make an edible shelter! Cattails are almost entirely edible (see the cattail section in chapter six). The non-edible parts can be used for cordage, weaving, basket materials, and even arrow shafts!

Cattail debris hut

Building a debris hut, step 1

Building a debris hut, step 2

Building a debris hut, step 3

Building a debris hut, step 5

simple framework of sticks and then piling forest debris on top of it. It's also important to stuff the inside with debris as well to help retain heat. I've slept in debris huts in temperatures as low as 40°F (4°C) with debris piled 2'–3' (1m) thick on the outside of the framework. They've not been my most comfortable nights of sleep, but I lived. Here's how I build a debris hut:

Step 1: Using two Y sticks and one long, center ridge pole, create a framework long enough to contain your body.

Step 2: Lean a framework of sticks against the center ridge pole 1"–3" (3–8cm) apart to create a sturdy roof area.

Step 3: Pile on a bunch of smaller branches, briars, or brambles that will hold the debris in place as you dump it on.

Step 4: Keep piling until the frame is covered with 2'–3' (1m) of debris—the more debris, the warmer the hut.

Step 5: Fill the inside with debris and crawl inside. Be sure to plug the

Pine needle debris hut

Mag's and Finnick's Lean-To Shelter

In warmer weather, you can build a lean-to style shelter similar to the one Mags and Finnick weave out of grass during the Quarter Quell. This type of shelter offers little warmth, but will protect against wind, rain, and dew.

Lean-tos are the quintessential survival shelter and are by far the easiest to erect. It's really as simple as leaning a framework of poles against a ridge line and then covering that roof with bark, leafy branches, grass, or a combination of all three.

I've never been a big fan of using complicated weaving and thatching methods to create a roof because, quite frankly, I don't plan on staying in any survival shelter for too long, and that's a lot of energy and time to spend for only a few nights of shelter.

One good rule to remember when building lean-to shelters is to face the

door hole with debris to prevent heat loss out the front of the shelter.

I've also build a debris hut mainly using cattail plants from a nearby pond. It poured down rain when I slept in this shelter and only a few drips came inside.

Lean-to framework

Lean-to framework with roof

slanted roof toward the wind and the open wall areas away from the wind. This helps to keep wind from blowing directly into your shelter—the top is both a roof and a wind screen.

The finished lean-to with grass roof photo is what I imagine Mags and Finnick's grass lean-to would look like. I've used a fallen tree to create a shallow-roofed lean-to. This style is very simple to create and also provides protection from two sides. One of the other open walls can easily be covered with a pile of sticks, leaves or branches. Rain is not coming through this roof.

The photo of the heavy duty lean-to shows a larger and steeper version of a lean-to shelter. The general concept is the same. Instead of grasses, I've used leafy branches to cover the roof. A few more to go, and this roof will be nearly water-tight.

After your roofing material, whether it's grass or leaves, is in place, it's a good idea to add a few heavier branches on top to keep the roof in

Finished lean-to with grass roof

Heavy duty lean-to

place in case the wind picks up. I learned this the hard way—in the middle of the night during a mild storm—years ago.

Mother Nature will provide you with many lean-to thatching materials in temperate months. Tall grasses, like those pictured, are excellent streamlined "roof shingles." Leafy branches, such as those found on maple trees, work equally as well. Pine boughs are also an effective roofing material. If you are lucky enough to locate some large-leaf plants, such as wild skunk cabbage or burdock (also edible), it may only take a few handfuls of tennis-racquet-sized leaves to waterproof an entire lean-to shelter. Second to man-made materials, these are some of the best waterproofing plants I've used.

KATNISS'S PLASTIC TARP

You might be lucky enough to find or scavenge man-made shelter materials when you're in a survival scenario. I would be remiss not to mention the 3' (1m) square sheet of plastic (a tarp) that Katniss uses in her first Hunger Games. In nature, you won't find anything that can waterproof like a simple plastic tarp. I will discuss the many different survival uses for a plastic tarp several times throughout the book, but for now, let's focus on how it can be used for sheltering.

The large leaves of burdock make excellent roofing materials

Grove of wild skunk cabbage, enough "shingles" for a hundred lean-tos

Lean-to shelter using skunk cabbage leaves

Completed skunk cabbage lean-to

Katniss's 3' (1m) square sheet of plastic

Post bed with plastic ground cover and leaves for insulation material

Salvaging a plastic tarp—what a *huge score*! Though smaller than I'd prefer, a 3' (1m) square piece of plastic is an awesome piece of kit when it comes to survival shelter. It can be used in a number of ways. When it comes to shelter, here are my top three uses for the tarp:

1. Shelter Canopy

The first and most practical shelter use is as an overhead canopy—or partial canopy because of the size. Use cordage to secure the tarp to the frame of either a debris hut or lean-to, then place the natural-found roofing materials on top of the plastic. If your tarp is as short as Katniss's, position the plastic above the space where you will rest your head and body core (torso). The tarp will repel rain and help keep warmth inside the shelter by reflecting body heat in cold-weather scenarios when it's important to keep your core warm.

2. Ground Cover

Con·duc·tion [kuhn-duhk-shuhn]: noun, the transfer of heat between substances that are in direct contact with each other.

The cold, hard ground will suck the life-sustaining warmth right out of you if you let it. If the ground is moist, you'll lose even more body heat at a much faster rate. A sheet of plastic makes an excellent moisture barrier when used as a ground cover. That isn't enough, though. The plastic only protects from moisture and will do nothing against cold. You must pile a layer of insulation on top of the plastic. You can use a huge variety of materials including:

- Grasses
- Hay
- Leaves—dead or green
- Pine boughs (any evergreen works great)
- Corn shucks
- Cattails

The combination of the plastic and the insulation will make for a very efficient (and comfortable) ground cover that will rival any store-bought sleeping pad. Containing the insulation material between two staked logs makes an even more effective sleeping "bed" by keeping the material in place beneath you during the night.

3. Wind Block

The wind is like a thief in the night, and it is only interested in stealing your warmth. In a cold-weather scenario, building a screen to block the wind can be a big help. Of course, this can be done with natural materials, such as stacked logs, but this stack will still have leaks and drafts. Wind can't pass through a plastic tarp, so there will be no drafts, and you'll notice the cutting effects of cold air flow are more drastically reduced.

Stacked log wind screen

Two long stakes rolled three times on each side

Sharpened ends staked in the ground to form an upright wind block

I've found the easiest way to set up a quick wind screen with a small plastic sheet is to roll up opposite sides of the sheet with two long stakes and then stake it where you need it. Violà, instant wall.

SUMMARY

Don't overcomplicate shelter. It can be a very time-consuming and calorie-sucking task if you let the grandeur of a shelter you've seen in a movie cloud your judgment. Shelter is about *function,* period. It doesn't have to look pretty, and no one is going to judge your design skills. Remember the basics. If a squirrel with a pea-sized brain can do it, then so can you.

THREE

HYDRATION: HAYMITCH SAYS "FIND A WATER SOURCE"

IN THEIR LAST MOMENTS before entering the arena, Peeta asks Haymitch for some words of advice. Without hesitation, Haymitch responds with two simple commands: *run away* and then *find a water source*. Haymitch is right, finding a water source should be at the *top* of your survival priority list. Remember, in extreme conditions you can only live for three days without water. Dehydration can debilitate you quickly, as Katniss learns early in her first Hunger Games. The dry mouth, headaches, and sensitive eyesight she experiences are all very real symptoms of dehydration. Over 70 percent of the human body is water. Even a small percentage of water loss can have devastating consequences. Yes, you can live three days without water, but after the first twenty-four hours without water you are going to be pretty miserable. After forty-eight hours, you'll be crippled with cramps, light-headed, and weak. Soon after, you'll begin to hallucinate and major organs will slowly begin to fail you. If you wait too long, it might be too late. Don't wait until you are dehydrated to hunt for water. If you are thirsty, you are already dehydrated.

LET NATURE BE YOUR GUIDE

While searching for water, Katniss relies on natural signs to guide her path. She's a smart girl and knows a thing or two about finding survival water. Her time in the woods has paid off. What does she know about how to find water? What can we learn by observing her?

Water Travels Downhill

Water takes the easiest route available (the path of least resistance) and travels downhill. Gravity causes

The still-damp outside bend of a dried-up stream

Water collected in a cup formed by the leaves of a plant

Water in a solid rock depression

Small game animal trail

Animal den

water to find its way from high places, like snowy mountaintops, to low places, like lake beds and valleys. Your first move toward water should be downhill.

Running water will cut a groove in the earth—even in solid rock. There may not be running water where you are, but grooves in the earth's surface may lead you to where it went. As it snakes its way downhill in search of a resting place in some kind of depression, water leaves tracks just like animals. That depression can be a stump at the base of a tree, a divot in a rock canyon, a pond at the base of a mountain, a deep corner pool in the bend of a shallow stream, or even the largest depression on earth—the ocean.

Even dried-up streams can yield water. Damp outside bends in a dried-up riverbed may still have ground water beneath the surface. If you dig a hole, called a seepage well (detailed later), in these areas, ground water may seep into it for you to collect.

All Living Things Need Water

Living things can lead you to water. You aren't the only one whose survival depends on water. Water gives life to everything from plants to animals.

Animals: At one point in her search, Katniss hopes to spot a game trail that might lead her to water. A

Animal scat

Animal tracks

game trail is simply a path created by an animal (in hunting, *game* is the term used for the animal you are after). Animals seek the easiest routes to wherever they are going and they often follow the same path from their dens or nests to their feeding and watering grounds, thus creating a trail. Almost all game trails lead either to or from a food or water source. If you find an animal game trail, you are not far from water. Follow it, preferably downhill. While you are at it, set a snare on the trail as well. Don't worry, we cover how to set Gale's famous twitch-up snares later on in chapter six.

A nest, burrow, or den is a good sign that water isn't far off. Animals follow the survival rule you learned in chapter two: build shelter near resources (food and water). Try to follow a trail leading away from an animal's home. There's a good chance it leads to water.

Other signs of animal activity may also be indicators. Tracks, scat, or rubs can indicate animals are traveling through the area. You must try your best to read every detail of the landscape.

Vegetation: Lush, green vegetation is a sign of water. Plants will grow wherever there is water, even in the middle of the most barren deserts on earth. Scan the horizon and look for patches of growth that seem

YOUR SPONSOR HAS SENT YOU A

SURVIVAL QUICK TIP

Inspect any scat (animal poo) you might find to get an idea of what your prey is already eating. You can use this information when baiting traps.

SURVIVAL QUICK TIP

The sycamore tree typically grows near water. Sycamore trees can be a sign that you are coming close to water source. The sycamore is easy to identify by its unmistakable bark coloring and pattern. It looks like winter camouflage with a white base and tan camo patterns. The photo shows a sycamore leaf against its very unique bark.

Sycamore leaf and bark

better nourished. Spotting a green oasis from afar can save you hours of searching. It may be very subtle, with growth slightly more abundant and colorful, but areas with water *will* look different from areas without it.

BIOLOGICAL THREATS IN WATER

You've finally found water, but don't take a big gulp just yet. Simply finding water is only half of the hydration equation. Water can save your life, but it can also turn you into a barfing, cramping, aching, dying messpile of a person. It is *drinkable water* that is the key. There are two kinds of survival water: water that needs to be purified and water that doesn't. The devil is in the details and it is critical

that you know the difference. Your life depends on it.

Unfortunately, your water-born enemies are invisible to the naked eye. It's biological threats (micro-organisms) that are your greatest water threat in a wilderness environment. Other threats include hazardous pollutants and heavy metals, which are more of a concern in large cities like the Capitol. Ingesting water infected with nasty little living critters can quickly turn your insides into a gastrointestinal nightmare. From vomiting and cramping to diarrhea, thirst will quickly become the least of your worries. Without medical attention, your chances of surviving the effects of drinking contaminated water would be remote at best. There are three categories of biological threats in water:

- **Protozoan Cysts:** These are the largest of the three but still invisible to the naked eye. They include things like Giardia and Cryptosporidium.
- **Bacteria:** These guys are slightly smaller than cysts and include popular critters, such as E. coli, salmonella, and cholera.
- **Viruses:** The smallest of the three, this lovely grouping includes some real winners like hepatitis A and polio.

Needless to say, you don't want to take a gulp of any of them. Like I said, there are two categories of survival water: water that needs to be purified (because it might be contaminated with one of the three threats above) and water that doesn't need to be purified. Here's how you can tell the difference.

WATER THAT NEEDS TO BE PURIFIED

I have to give Katniss major kudos. She exercises some serious discipline when it comes to disinfecting her drinking water. Even when she is at the brink of death from dehydration, she knows the importance of water purification. She is lucky enough to have some iodine that could be used to purify water in the arena. We'll get into to how to use iodine to purify water shortly.

Basically, any open water source that you find in nature needs to be purified. This includes water sourced from ponds, streams, crevices, open pits, holes, puddles, rivers, lakes and hollow stumps. If it has had the opportunity to touch the earth, an animal or an insect, then it should be purified. Though still not safe to drink, running water is considered "safer" than non-moving, stagnant water. If collecting water from a stagnant pool is your only option, there is a survival method for getting the best you can from this source—that's the seepage well.

Seepage Well

A seepage well is a hole dug in the ground at least 3' (1m) from the edge of the stagnant water source. You may have to dig the hole as much as 3' (1m) deep. When you dig this hole, water will slowly filter through the soil and fill the well. The soil will help to filter out insect larvae and other larger contaminants. Allow this water to sit in the well for several hours so that sediments sink to the bottom. You can then collect water from the top. This water will still need to be purified. You can also use this method to gather water in dried-up, but still damp, riverbeds. While water might

Seepage well in the middle of a muddy forest floor with no other water in sight

The same seepage well thirty minutes later

not be visible on the surface, ground water will often flow into a seepage well if dug in damp areas.

WATER PURIFICATION METHODS FOR SURVIVAL SITUATIONS

OK, so you've found water in one of the sources mentioned above. Now, you have to purify it. I often hear people use the words *purify* and *filter* interchangeably, as if they mean the same thing. These are *not* the same thing. Purification kills all germs but filtration only filters out some germs. Many store-bought water filters are sufficient at filtering out the nasties and further purification isn't required. The Katadyn Hiker Pro pump filter is one that I use regularly on backpacking and camping trips, and it works great.

Improvising a filter of this quality isn't realistic in a wilderness survival scenario. But filtering does still have its place in a survivor's bag of water tricks. Sometimes the water you find will need to be prefiltered before you attempt to purify it. In a perfect world, you will be able to find nice, clean, clear-flowing water. In the real world, there are rarely perfect scenarios. Water you collect from nature can be full of floating debris, mud, insects, sticks, and anything else you can imagine. It is ideal to prefilter this water. Your prefilter doesn't have to be fancy. You can use a bandana, a sock, a T-shirt, or even a mass of dried grasses. Simply pour the water through one of these items to crudely filter out large floating debris and sediment.

Boiling

Bringing water to a rolling boil (large bubbles that come all the way to the top of the water and break the sur-

Katadyn Hiker Pro water filter

Pouring water through dried grasses

Pouring water through a bandana

face) will kill all biological threats. However, boiling has some drawbacks. First, you must have a heat source—a fire or some kind of stove and fuel. Assuming you have a heat source hot enough to boil water, you then need a container that won't be destroyed by the heat (typically this means you need a metal container). It could be hard to come by either of these (heat source or container) in a wilderness survival scenario you're not prepared for. To boil water, there's no alternative to a heat source, but there is an alternative if you are missing a metal container.

Boiling: Katniss's Rock-Heated Soup

At one point during her time in the arena, Katniss uses rocks heated by the sun to warm a bowl of soup. She simply places the hot rocks right in the soup and they heat the soup with no problem. The same concept can be used to boil water if you don't have a container that can be placed directly on a heat source. Gather small rocks (about the size of golf balls) and place them in the coals of a fire. Obviously these stones will get extremely hot, some will even turn red, so how will you get these rocks out of the fire and into your water? Create makeshift tongs by splitting a *green* tree branch in half and then bending it in the middle.

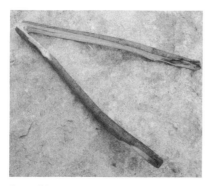

Carved tongs

Carved tongs placing hot rocks

Rocks boiling water in coal-burned container

Use the makeshift tongs to transfer the hot rocks a few at a time into a container of water. The heat of the rocks will bring the water to a boil. As boiling slows, take out the cooled rocks and replace them with newly heated ones. Do *not* return the stones to fire for reheating.

In the photos here, I have used fire to burn out a depression in a section of wood. (Coal-burned containers were commonly used by many primitive peoples; you'll learn how to make this type of container in chapter five.) After the cavity is large enough to hold water, hot rocks can be added to boil the water.

Chemical Purification: Katniss's Bottle of Iodine

Chemical purification is a very practical water treatment method. In fact, the vast majority of our city water is treated chemically with chlorine. If you know the tips and tricks, you can also purify water chemically in a survival situation. In the arena, Katniss is meticulous about purifying her water with iodine. Iodine has been used as a disinfectant since the early 1900s. As Katniss demonstrates several times throughout her stint in the arena, it is an excellent water purification chemical. The dosage is simple: 5 drops of 2 percent iodine tincture per liter of water. After adding the iodine, wait at least thirty minutes before drinking the water.

Even though chemicals can purify water, it's very important to remember that iodine is poisonous. A few drops in water will disinfect it, but even a tablespoon will harm you. Be very careful to use the minimum effective amount in your water. If possible, use a water container with units of measurement on it (liters and ounces) so you have the correct ratio of water to chemical.

I mention chemical purification as an option, because it is the method Katniss uses, but in a true survival situation, it's unlikely that you'll have access to iodine unless you carry a survival kit (discussed in chapter nine) with you or find one, as Katniss does. If you carry a survival kit, include chemical water purifica-

YOUR SPONSOR HAS SENT YOU A

SURVIVAL QUICK TIP

Only use rocks found in dry areas. Rocks found in wet areas can contain moisture, which could cause them to explode when heated. For this same reason, don't return the rocks to the fire after you've used them to heat your water.

tion tablets in it. They're designed for backpackers, so they are very small, inexpensive, and readily available at most outdoors stores. Best of all, these are premeasured and come with detailed instructions, so you'll know how to use them.

Ultraviolet Rays

We have a love-hate relationship with the sun. One day it's bad, the next day it's good. We need sunlight for warmth, light, and to grow plants, but we also are aware that overexposure to sunlight causes skin cancer. Solar power is an incredible resource, even in a survival situation. A very effective but time-consuming method of water purification is called solar water disinfection or SODIS for short. The concept is very simple and has

2 percent tincture of iodine found at any local pharmacy and in many household first aid kits

been endorsed by the World Health Organization and the Red Cross as a viable method of purifying water in developing countries. If you fill up a clear plastic or glass bottle (or even bag) with water and leave it in direct sunlight for six consecutive hours, the UVA rays will kill any biological threats. There are a few guidelines that must be followed to make this method effective:

- The container must be fully exposed to a minimum of six hours of full sun.
- The water must be clear, not murky or cloudy (see prefiltering techniques mentioned earlier).
- The container must hold less than three liters of water.
- The container must be clear, not tinted.
- PET bottles are recommended. (Look for the PET labeling on the bottle.)

For more information about solar water disinfection, visit the website www.sodis.ch/index_EN.

Worst-Case Scenario Survival Filter

In a worst-case scenario, if you have no other purification options you can improvise a makeshift survival water filter as a last-ditch effort. This type of filter is not guaranteed to remove all water-borne threats, but it would be

better than nothing at all. I call it the Tre-Filter. (*Tre* is Swedish for three.) The Tre-Filter is a three-layer improvised filter that can be constructed in a huge variety of ways—your creativity and available resources are the limit. The three key ingredients are:

- dried grass
- sand
- charcoal

In the sample shown in the photos, I've made a Tre-Filter using a discarded two-liter plastic soda bottle.

Step 1: Cut off the bottom of the bottle and place a bunch of dried grasses in the bottle's neck. This wad of grasses (called the plug) prevents everything above it from falling through the mouth of the bottle.

Step 2: Pile on a layer of crushed charcoal. You can get charcoal from

Grass plug with charcoal on top

Sand layer added

Hanging Tre-Filter

your fire pit. After your fire has cooled, there will be small chunks of black charcoal. This is charred wood that hasn't burned all the way into ash. Ashes are not charcoal. Simply crush up the charcoal using a rock. Charcoal has excellent absorbing properties and is an important component of many modern filtering systems.

Step 3: Above the charcoal, add a layer of sand.

Step 4: On top of the sand, place a layer of dried grasses, which serves as a crude filter layer to remove larger floating debris. You can also use a T-shirt or bandana as this top-most layer.

Simply pour water into the top and let it filter down through the layers and out the bottom hole. But remember, using a Tre-Filter is still risky. It's not guaranteed to remove microscopic biological threats. Use this method only as a last option.

WATER THAT DOESN'T NEED TO BE PURIFIED

Gathering water that doesn't need to be purified is certainly preferred. It saves time, fuel, and energy. Finding fresh drinking water is certainly not a guarantee, but sure is nice.

Keeping in the theme of energy conservation, here's a list of the most practical methods for gathering water that does not need to be purified, starting with the easiest.

Tarp as rain catch canopy

Dug hole lined with plastic garbage bag to collect rain water

Rain

Rain can be collected and consumed without treatment or purification. However, you need to collect it in your own container. As soon as rainwater comes in contact with the earth or another water source (e.g., puddle, pond, stream), it needs to be purified. So what's the best way to collect the rainwater without having it touch the ground? If you set your container out in the rain and just waited for it fill, it would take a very long time to fill up (if it ever does).

The most effective way to gather rainwater is to build a rain-catch system. If possible, use a tarp, plastic sheet, garbage bag, or rain jacket to capture and funnel rain water into one or more containers. Katniss's 3' (1m) square plastic sheet is a perfect tool for improvising a makeshift rain-catch system. Lining a hole in the

ground or depression is an excellent makeshift survival container and can often hold more water than smaller containers.

You can also use natural materials from nonpoisonous trees and plants to collect rainwater. Bark is excellent for funneling and directing

Oak bark leaning against a simple tripod to help funnel water into plastic-lined hole

water towards larger collection areas. Large leaves can also be used to increase collection surface area and to direct water into containers. Every square inch of surface area is important when you might need every last drop of water to stay alive.

No survival scenario is the same. The only constants that remain the same from situation to situation are the principles behind the skills that work. As long as you understand basic survival principles, you will be able to improvise a working solution. With rain collection, the survival principle you need to understand is *increased surface area.*

Snow

In the arena, Katniss mentions that she sometimes melts snow to drink back at home. If you try this, use only

YOUR SPONSOR HAS SENT YOU A

SURVIVAL QUICK TIP

Burdock is an amazing wild edible plant. It is a cultivated crop in some countries and the roots are sold in many high-end organic heath food stores.

snow that is fresh and white. The chances that snow is contaminated increase the longer the snow sits on whatever surface it has landed on.

The old survival adage of "Don't eat snow!" is true. Eating snow can sap valuable energy through your digestive system. In a cold-weather environment, you need to hang on

A large leaf shelter canopy doubles for rain collection when "bark gutters" at the base direct run-off to a desired area

Burdock leaves used to increase surface area and direct rain into bottle placed in a hole in the ground

Snow-Kabob melting next to fire

Snow melting in sock near fire

to every last calorie. If possible, melt snow before you consume it. Four proven ways to effectively melt snow for drinking are:

1. **Metal Container:** Melting snow in a metal container over heat (fire) is the fastest way to melt snow for drinking. Many metal containers will work, including baking pans, makeshift tin foil cups, wheel hubcaps, coffee cans, or even soda cans.

2. **Drip 'n Sip:** Place snow in a cloth bag, bandana, or sock and hang it next to a fire. Position a container so that the melting snow drips into it. The cloth wrap also acts as a crude filter.

3. **Snow-Kabob:** Skewer a snowball onto a spiked stick positioned next to a fire. Allow the melting snow to drip into a container.

4. **Snow Buddy:** If no heat source is available, pack a container with snow and place it under your cloths close to your body. Your body heat will slowly melt the snow. This will also suck away your body heat and should be considered a last resort.

 YOUR SPONSOR HAS SENT YOU A

SURVIVAL QUICK TIP

- Unlike snow, ice must be purified before drinking.
- Our kidneys cannot properly process the salt in sea water. Drinking water from the ocean actually accelerates dehydration.

Dew

At night when temperatures drop, moisture in the air condenses and collects on exposed surfaces. This is what we commonly refer to as *dew*. Dew accumulates in surprisingly large amounts each morning, even on blistering hot days. The dew that collects on grass and vegetation is considered perfectly fine to drink. The trick is gathering it. Have you ever walked through dew-soaked grass? What happens? Your shoes and pants get soaked, right? Collecting dew is surprisingly simple and incredibly effective. I've collected a gallon of dew in less than one hour. The process is simple: Walk through as much dewy grass as possible and ring out the dew into a container. Tie off as many items as you can to your lower legs—bandanas, T-shirts, towels, etc. The more dew you can soak up, the faster you can gather it. Hurry, though; dew evaporates quickly, and then you have to wait another twenty-four hours.

WATER FROM PLANTS AND TREES

The Quarter Quell in *Catching Fire* is a sober reminder of how dehydration can be an issue to a survivor even when she is completely surrounded by water. Ocean water actually harms our bodies more than it helps them; only fresh water will provide proper hydration. The tributes fend off dehydration by tapping trees for drinkable sap (detailed next). Our primitive survivor ancestors used plants and trees as water resources for thousands of years. Here are a few ways they used them.

Tapping Trees

Maple trees have been tapped for centuries for their sap, which is boiled

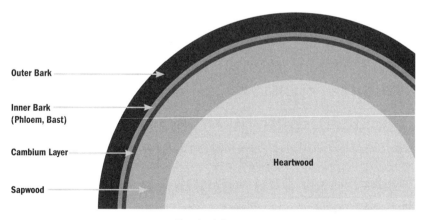

Tree bark layers

Close up of spile

Carved out hole with horsetail spile

down to make maple syrup. The reason it has to be boiled is to remove all of the water contained in the sap. Forty gallons of maple sap yields only one gallon of maple syrup—that's how much water is in the sap! Sap from nonpoisonous trees is 100 percent drinkable and also contains sugar and nutrients from the tree. Look at it as nature's version of an energy drink. In late winter and early spring, many trees will gush sap if you cut into the sapwood layer.

Katniss does just this when Haymitch sends her a spile. A spile is the tool used to drain out sap from trees during maple syrup production. It's basically a small tube that's inserted into a hold drilled about 1" (25mm) into the side of a maple tree.

Some trees, like the maple, will drain sap almost all year round; the sap just moves a lot slower in sum-

mer and fall than in winter and early spring. In the Eastern Woodlands of the United States, the best trees for sap are: maple, birch, hickory and sycamore. Maple and birch are the best in my experience.

It's not likely that you will have a spile (or a drill to make a hole) handy in a survival situation. Don't let that stop you. With a little effort, you can carve a hole into a tree with a pocketknife or even an improvised tool. A hollow piece of reed grass, horsetail, or bamboo can suffice as a natural alternative to a spile.

A crude "sap wedge" can be made by carving a V-shaped notch at least a ½" (12mm) into the tree. The sap will seep to the bottom of the V. Placing a piece of leaf at this intersection will act as a wick, and with a little finesse the sap will drip from the tip of the leaf into a container below.

Reed grass, horsetail and bamboo sections

Sap V-shaped wedge

First-year bull thistle plant

Bull Thistle

Bull thistle is the American Midwest version of a cactus. It is an invasive plant that is very common in much of the country. What many people don't realize is that the bull thistle is covered with thorns to protect a very precious and valuable resource: *water*. The bull thistle holds more water than any other plant in the Midwest. Its thick, lush center stalk is full of water-packed cells. After the prickly outside skin and leaves have been carved away, you can eat the inner pulp raw or squeeze the water from it. Just as apple cider is pressed from apples, thistle juice can be pressed from thistles. It has a very weedy flavor but is completely fine to drink.

The best way to harvest the bull thistle pulp is to carve off all the leaves and spines while the plant is still standing. It's easy to work your way around the plant this way. After the coast is clear, simply whack off the stalk and slice off the bitter outer rind to access the inner pulp.

Grapevines

In North America, wild grapevines are prevalent in almost every forest area. The leaves and curly tendrils are tell-tale ways to identify the vine.

Grapevines are known to contain a crazy amount of fresh drinking water. I've harvested over a gallon of

Grape leaf

Water collected from draining a grape-vine for twenty minutes

water from one grapevine. Cut the grapevine off near the ground and let it drain into a container. Let it sit for a while even if there are no immediate results. Do not drink the liquid from vines if it's milky, white, stinks, or tastes bitter. Vine water should be fresh smelling and fairly clear.

Natural Plant Catches

Plants are survivors. Many plants are shaped and designed to funnel rainfall and water toward the center and down to the roots. Occasionally, with astute observation, you will notice that some plants will actually hold water in what I call Natural Plant Catches. This is more common in large-leaf plants. The intersection of their leaves and stalk can sometime form a cup that holds rainwater long after the last rain. Be aware that

these occurrences do exist and take the time to quickly glance at bases of large-leaf plants.

Transpiration Bag

Transpiration is to plants as sweating is to humans. Leaves of plants and trees release moisture into the air. If

YOUR SPONSOR HAS SENT YOU A

SURVIVAL QUICK TIP

When collecting water from vines, make a slice in the vine about 5'-6' (2m) above where you've cut it off. This helps to speed the flow. This acts as a breather valve, similar to one on a gas can.

we can speed up this process and then capture that moisture from the leaves of nonpoisonous plants and trees, the resulting water you collect does not require purification. It just so happens that there is a survival technique for capturing this "transpired water." It's called a transpiration bag. It requires a clear and fairly thin plastic bag. (Or even a sheet of plastic like the one Katniss finds! Yes, there is yet another use for that plastic sheet! It's so simple but so multifunctional.)

Building a transpiration bag is incredibly simple. It does require full (and hot) sun. Simply wrap a branch full of leaves inside the bag and tie it off at the base. Place a small rock in the bottom corner to create a low spot for water to collect. This must be done in *full sun*. Southward facing branches will received the most sun

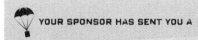
throughout the day. The sun's rays will speed up transpiration, which will be trapped by the bag and then collect in the corner with the rock weight. It will take several hours for water to collect. Simply untie the base and pour the water into a container or drink it right out of the bag. Don't be alarmed if it is discolored or tastes a little like leaves; this is normal. I've

Transpiration bag on leafy maple branch

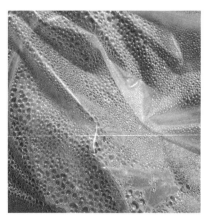

Close-up of moisture collecting on the inside of a transpiration bag

Building a solar still, step 1

Building a solar still, step 2

Building a solar still, step 3

Building a solar still, step 4

had excellent results using this technique with both maple and willow trees.

Solar Still

The much more labor-intensive cousin of the transpiration bag is the solar still. You can still use leaves and vegetation in a solar still and capitalize on transpiration. However, a solar still also works by collecting evaporating water that isn't necessarily inside plants. It is the most basic form of distillation. Pure water can be distilled from sea water and even urine. When collected, this water is pure and clean to drink. Again, the solar still requires full, hot sun exposure to work effectively. Floating solar stills are kept in life raft survival kits and can be used to distill drinking water from salty sea water. Building a survival solar still is pretty basic.

Step 1: Dig a hole in the ground approximately 30" (76cm) in diameter × 30" (76cm) deep.

Step 2: Line the hole with lush (nonpoisonous) vegetation. You can pour in some sea water or urinate in the hole. The ground also contains moisture. Place a clean container in the very center of the hole. In this example I used a disposable plastic drinking cup.

Step 3: Place a flexible tube in the container that leads out of the hole (optional).

Step 4: Cover the hole loosely with clear plastic and seal the edges with rocks, dirt, or sand. Place a small rock in the middle to create a low point in the plastic just above the container.

Moisture inside of the hole will evaporate and collect on the clear plastic. That moisture will eventually form droplets of pure water that will drip into the container. The tube can be used to drink the water out of the container without breaking down the still. Don't expect an impressive

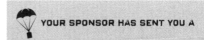

YOUR SPONSOR HAS SENT YOU A

SURVIVAL QUICK TIP

Don't chug your water! Your kidneys can only process 8 fluid ounces (237ml) of water every fifteen minutes. Pace yourself when rehydrating. Keeping with this schedule ensures the most efficient use of your precious water.

amount of water from one of these. The most I've ever gotten is just under a cup, but this method can be a way to supplement other water collection efforts.

SUMMARY

When it comes to survival water, you may not have one perfect fresh water source. Like Katniss, you might have to pull from a variety of resources to meet your daily hydration requirements. Remember, water can kill you just as fast as it can save you. Don't let extreme thirst cloud your judgment. Thirst is a sign that you are *already* dehydrated.

FOUR

CATCHING SURVIVAL FIRE

OUR ANCESTORS DEPENDED ON FIRE for survival. They used it to cook, keep warm and create useful tools. And even though we don't often *see* fire now, we are really no less dependent on fire in modern society. Fire-starting skills are critical to survival.

As Katniss and the other tributes show us, there are a number of ways you can use fire, both in the arena and real life, to meet a variety of survival needs including warmth, signaling, cooking and boiling, and making tools. But before we go any further, it's important to note that fire can be incredibly dangerous and destructive. If you're under the age of eighteen, don't attempt anything described in this chapter unless you have a responsible adult helping you. Fire is a tool, not a toy. You must respect it.

WARMTH

The most important function of fire is to regulate core body temperature, or help you stay warm! A nice, big fire can counteract the effects of even the most severe winter weather. In cold weather, when a shelter isn't enough to keep you warm, you must have fire to survive. In the arena, you never know what type of climate the Gamemaker will throw at you. The temperature can drop in a matter of minutes and you'll need to fight off hypothermia.

But be smart about how you build your fire. Remember what happened in the 74th Hunger Games? Building a fire can be one of the fastest ways to get a canon fired on your behalf. Not all fires have to give away your location. The Dakota fire hole, which I will discuss later, is a virtually invisible fire for those times when being seen might be a bad thing.

SIGNALING

Signal fires are a classic survival rescue signal. What is a signal fire? It's one that puts off heavy smoke

Warming by fire

Signal fire built with green leafy boughs for lots of smoke

Roasting squirrel over an open fire

Fire hardening spear point

during the day and bright flames at night. Signal fires are best built using green wood and leafy boughs. The more "alive" your fire material is, the more it will smoke. Dry material will smoke far less. Katniss makes good use of smoky signal fires on several occasions in the arena. You'd be smart to follow her example.

COOKING AND BOILING

From groosling to rabbit, to edible roots and wild greens, you'll find lots to eat in Panem. (We will discuss how to find and catch many of these in detail in chapter six). A warm meal will do a lot to sustain you in the arena, so you'll want to build a fire for cooking. Fire allows you to cook meat, smoke jerky, roast roots, steam greens, simmer stews, and most importantly, boil water. Boiling may be your only option for purifying dirty water. In this

case, your life could depend on getting fire within a three day time period so that you can purify and drink water before you die of dehydration.

MAKING TOOLS

Fire is at the center of almost every modern-day manufacturing process because it can transform and change raw materials unlike any other process. You can use fire to do amazing things. Native Americans started controlled fires in fields and then walked through the charred remains to eat the roasted grasshoppers and insects. Hot coals can be used to create coal-burned wooden containers that can be used for cooking and even boiling water (detailed in chapter three). Fire can burn through logs too large to move and also be used to harden carved spear and arrow points. Pine sap and charcoal can be heated and mixed to create an amazing natural epoxy, a glue-like substance. Fire is a powerful tool and can help transform other items into tools.

FIRE COMPONENTS

If you can't successfully build, start and maintain a fire, you can't benefit from all of its uses. Peeta is very good at starting fires because of all his experience in the bakery. Mastering fire building *only* comes from experience. It's a survival skill you'll need to practice (in a safe, controlled environment with parental supervision if you're under eighteen) before you enter the arena (or encounter a survival situation).

In addition to experience, you need two items to build a fire: fire tinder (the fuel) and ignition source (the heat). Heat + Fuel + Oxygen = Fire. In a previous Hunger Games, many of the tributes froze to death because there was no wood to build a fire. If you have nothing to burn, you can't keep a fire going. This section will show you multiple options for fuels and ignition sources so you can start a fire in almost any situation.

Fire Tinder

A tinder bundle is the very first fire-starting material you will try to ignite when building a fire. It should be the finest, driest, lightest, and most combustible gathering of materials you can get your hands on. An ideal tinder bundle is:

- **Dry! Dry! Dry!** The only exception is when your tinder is mixed with an extender or accelerant, which I'll discuss later.
- **Fibrous:** Thin fibers burn easily and quickly; the more hair-thin fibers the better.
- **Not too small:** Some tinder bundles can go up in smoke pretty fast. If your bundle is too small, your window of opportunity to get other more substantial kindling materials lit is very short. I always try to start with a tinder bundle at least the size of a softball if possible.

A tinder bundle has one purpose: to catch a spark or flame and burn hot enough long enough to ignite larger kindling pieces. I believe the test of a truly worthy tinder bundle is one that can catch on fire with just a spark or ember (such as from a fire by friction set, ferro rod, or flint and steel). If it requires the use of an open flame, such as a match or lighter, then it is lacking in one of the qualities above.

When you're trying to build a good fire, you'll do 99 percent of the work before you cast a single spark. The most important moments of the fire-building process are the first sixty seconds of flame. Nine times out of ten, the quality of your tinder bundle will determine whether or not your fire catches and grows. Preparation is everything. How well you prepare your fire-building materials before you start the fire will determine your rate of success, plain and simple.

In wet, windy, or any other not-so-perfect fire-building conditions, building a good tinder bundle will help you a lot. If you lack experience in finding, creating, or using tinder bundles, this section will help to lay the solid foundation you need.

When it comes to tinder materials, your creativity is the limit. Tinder materials can pretty much be divided into three categories. The first category applies only to real-world fire-building and survival situations. The second and third categories can be used in the real world, and will likely be your only option in Panem and the arena.

Store-bought fire tinder: There is *nothing* wrong with buying fire tinder products. There are some amazing products on the market that I highly recommend for survival kits, emergency kits, and Bug Out Bags. One product, for example, is called WetFire. This material's flammability is absolutely unreal. It will even catch a spark and burn while floating in

BUG OUT BAG

A Bug Out Bag is a self-contained kit designed to get your through seventy-two hours of independent survival while traveling from the scene of a disaster to a safe location. See chapter nine for more on Bug Out Bags.

water. I keep a few cubes of WetFire in every single survival kit I own, including my Bug Out Bag.

Other great store-bought tinders are called Tinder-Quik and Spark-Lite. These compact fire tinder tabs are treated with some kind of chemical accelerant, and they are very effective.

Some other materials that also work as excellent tinder in even the worst conditions are:

- Steel wool
- Magnesium bars
- Light My Fire TinderDust

If you are able to produce any kind of spark or ember, these store-bought tinders I've mentioned above will pretty much guarantee you a fire. I highly suggest packing one or more in your survival and emergency kits. One cube of WetFire is a part of my daily Every Day Carry (EDC). I carry it packed into a pill case on my keychain.

WetFire brand fire tinder burning in water

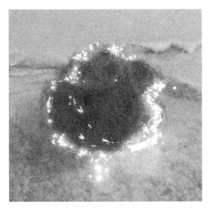

Steel wool smoldering from just a spark

Homemade dryer lint PET Balls

However, if you are ever in a situation when you aren't so fortunate to have store-bought fire tinder available, such as being in the arena, you will need to rely on your ability to improvise and scavenge for good tinder. This is when understanding the qualities of a good tinder bundle really come into play.

Homemade/Scavenged Fire Tinders (Non-Natural): One of the most reliable fire tinders I've ever used is a homemade product—cotton balls or dryer lint mixed with petroleum jelly. I call them PET Balls. Cotton balls, cotton pads, and dryer lint are the perfect tinder bundle consistency—extremely fibrous. The cotton balls by themselves are extremely flammable, but they burn really fast when lit. The petroleum jelly acts as a *fire extender*. It basically becomes a fuel that enables the flame to burn longer. I will discuss fire extenders and accelerants later.

So, what are other items that could be scavenged that have similar properties to cotton balls? Here are a few that come to mind:

- Dryer lint (or collected lint from your pockets)
- Unraveled fibrous rope or twine, such as jute twine
- Gauze bandages
- Tampons and maxi-pads
- Diapers
- Cigarette filters

YOUR SPONSOR HAS SENT YOU A

SURVIVAL QUICK TIP

In a pinch, you can even make lint by scraping a pair of denim jeans with the edge of a knife blade at a 90-degree angle. Lint will begin to accumulate and you can collect it and use as tinder.

Lint scraped from jeans

Char cloth is another excellent homemade fire tinder. Char cloth is made by charring 100 percent cotton cloth. I explain how to make your own char cloth in chapter five. Most papers can be rubbed and twisted into a fuzzy ball of excellent tinder material. Depending on the type of paper you have, it may take a little working, but it can be done. Paper is in essence a bunch of small fibers matted together. Fabric is also woven of small fibers and threads.

Once you understand the key properties of the tinder bundle, you can start to think about things and products in terms of whether or not they have potential to be good tinder materials. "Bushing" fire tinder between the palms of your hands helps

Bushing fire tinder between hands to fluff it up

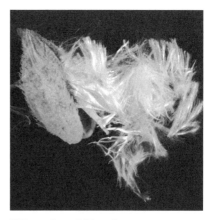

Milkweed seed "down"

to break it up and expose the small fibers that are so important.

Natural-Found Fire Tinders: If you know where to look, Mother Nature can provide you with amazing fire tinders no matter the season. The list of natural-found tinders can go on for pages. While I will give you specific natural materials that have worked for me, it's not important that you know these exactly. It's important that you understand the similar

Dried seed head from unknown plant

characteristics that make these items good fire tinders. No matter where you are in the world, plants and natural materials can be found and used as fire tinder. Knowing the attributes and not necessarily the name is what is important. With a few key exceptions, think *fluffy* and *fibrous*.

Dried seed heads from both plants and trees are often perfect tinder candidates. Even in the spring and summer months, many dried seed heads can still be found from the previous fall and winter season.

Cattail down

Little critters can also manufacture some excellent tinder bundles for you if you know where to look. You'll find that birds and other small animals are very picky about nesting materials and choose only the finest and softest twigs and leaves. These choice items just happen to be perfect for catching a spark or ember. Often, bird nests will dry quickly because

Bird nest fire tinder

Dry rodent nest

Birch bark fire tinder

of the high exposure to winds. Even when the ground is wet, I've found dry bird nests nestled in bushes and trees.

Small rodent nests also make awesome tinder bundles. These are typically hidden under logs or brush-piles, or even in a small underground burrow. Even though they can take a little work to find, they are almost always dry. Rodents don't like to sleep in a wet nest and go out of their way to build it in a dry area. With a little effort, you can uncover a dry tinder bundle rodent nest even in a down-pour of rain.

Several tree barks make excellent fire tinder as well. Birch bark is one of the best tinder materials on the planet and will light with a spark even when damp. The oil in the birch bark is ex-tremely flammable.

The resinous bark of a cedar tree also makes excellent tinder. I've found the best way to collect this is to scrape the bark with your knife at a 90-degree angle. This scrapes the bark off in almost a "fuzzy" consis-tency, which is perfect for catching a spark. A little effort goes a long way. Further rubbing cedar scrapings be-tween the palms of your hands helps to bring out the thin fibers.

Flame Extenders and Accelerants: Mixing fire tinder with a little bit of something flammable will drastically increase your odds of getting a flame going. There are two basic categories here: *extenders* and *accelerants*. Ex-tenders burn slow and steady. Accel-erants are more volatile and tend to burn very fast.

Some sample fire extenders are:
- Chapstick or lip balm
- Petroleum jelly
- Many hair pomades
- Fat (lard, grease, or rendered animal fat)

YOUR SPONSOR HAS SENT YOU A

SURVIVAL QUICK TIP

Wrap your lighters in duct tape. This not only helps make them more durable but duct tape also has many uses in a survival situation.

Disposable lighters

- Wax
- Pine sap

You will find that mixing your tinder with a fire extender will serve you two purposes:

1. Your spark will catch faster and better
2. Your flame will burn longer, giving you more time to catch small twigs and other kindling materials on fire

Fire accelerants, on the other hand, are much more explosive. Your spark will catch fast and your bundle will burn fast. Accelerants can really be helpful in the not-so-perfect situations, such as when it's wet and damp. Some example accelerants include:

- Gasoline
- Alcohol/hard liquor
- Perfumes
- Some mouthwashes

- Many cleaning supplies
- Hand sanitizer
- Tons of other chemical products, such as paint thinners

If you find yourself in an urban survival environment, like the one in *Mockingjay*, you might have access to a huge variety of fire accelerants. Use them to your advantage.

Ignition Source

The ignition source can be a flame, a spark, a chemical reaction, a burning ember or even intense heat hot enough to spontaneously combust flammable material. Katniss is lucky enough to find a box of wooden matches in her orange survival backpack. This is her ignition source. Not all tributes are that lucky. Many times you have to improvise. Here are some proven ignition devices:

Variety of ferrocerium rods

Ferro rod spraying sparks into tinder bundle

Disposable Lighters: In the real world, buy some cheap disposable cigarette lighters. They are typically only ninety-nine cents or so. Put one in *every* kit and backpack you own. Keep a few in your car, on your boat, and on any other mode of transportation you use. Pack them in your suitcases. Get in a habit of carrying one in your pocket as EDC. A ninety-nine cent cigarette lighter is the easiest way to start a fire.

Ferrocerium Rod: Ferrocerium is a man-made metal that gives off a shower of sparks when scraped with another blunt piece of metal, such as the back of a knife blade. It's very common in survival kits and is called a ferro rod, metal match, and "flint and steel" even though it is neither flint nor steel. Ferro rods can send off hot sparks even when soaking wet. The sparks are thousands of degrees in temperature and will quickly ignite most flammable fire tinders.

I carry a ferro rod in all of my survival kits and also keep one in

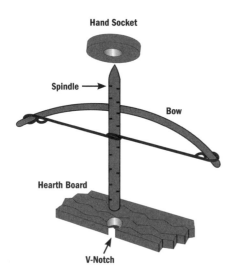

Bow-drill set schematic with labels

Hand Socket

Spindle

Bow

Hearth Board

V-Notch

my car. It's an indispensable piece of kit. Ferrocerium, though, cannot be found in nature and does not grow on trees. The next ignition device actually does grow on trees.

Friction Fire With Sticks: The bow-drill fire set. It doesn't get more primitive than rubbing two sticks together to make a fire. Making and using a bow-drill fire set is a lesson in both discipline and basic fire theory. It takes an intimate understanding of how fire works to take an ember generated from the friction of a bow drill and then blow that smoldering ember into a flame. There are several pieces of natural-found equipment you need to gather, modify and assemble:

The Spindle: First, create the spindle. This is the piece that spins

to create friction. It should be 8"–12" (20–30cm) long and about the diameter of your thumb. The top should be slightly pointed to reduce friction and the bottom should be carved more rounded to increase friction. The spindle needs to be straight and smooth. It should also be made from

Mullein plant

Yucca plant

a *bone dry* section of wood or woody stalked plant. My favorite spindle materials are from two plants: mullein and yucca. In the fall, the woody stalks from these plants die and dry out. I have also successfully used dried sticks from willow, tulip poplar, and cottonwood trees. I have not had success with hard woods, such as oak, hickory, or cherry.

The Bow: The bow should be made from a sturdy limb about as long as your arm. The ideal limb will have a slight curve. Many types of cordage will work for the bowstring—paracord, shoestring, hoodie drawstring, strip of leather, etc. When tying off the bowstring, leave enough slack to wrap the string around the spindle once. After the spindle is wrapped once, the bowstring should be very taught.

The Bearing Block: The bearing block is placed on top of the spindle

to apply pressure on the hearth board. Carve a notch or depression that fits the top of the spindle in the underside of the bearing block. In the photo, my bearing block is a chunk of walnut, but I've also used a rock, a shell, and even the root of a mullein plant.

The Hearth Board: The hearth board is the base wood that the spindle spins against to ultimately create an ember. This board also needs to be *bone dry*. I typically use the same wood as the spindle. The width

Spindle wrapped in bowstring

Walnut bearing block and hearth board

should not be smaller than the width of the spindle and the wood needs to be about ½–1" (12–25mm) thick.

You need to first carve a little starting depression in your hearth board about ¼" (6mm) from the edge.

To start the fire by friction process, use one foot to hold down the hearth board.

Wrap the cordage around the spindle. Place the spindle upright on the hearth board with the rounded end in the depression.

Carved depression

Place the bearing block on top of the spindle with the point resting in the notch or depression.

Put your hand firmly on top of the bearing block and keep your hand steady by bracing your wrist and forearm firmly against your shin as shown in the photo.

Use the bow to slowly spin the spindle while applying downward pressure with the bearing block. After a few seconds, you will see smoke as the spindle grooves out a larger hole for itself.

Starting position

When it starts to smoke, stop and carve a small pie-piece-shaped notch to the center of the newly burned depression. This notch allows the smoldering charred friction dust to collect and form a burning ember.

Before you start spinning the spindle again, place a "catch" under the notch. I often use a leaf, a wood

Carved notch with leaf "catch" in place

shaving, or a piece of leather as a catch. This catch allows you to safely remove the ember later and dump it into your tinder bundle.

Now, start spinning the spindle again, slow and steady at first. When it begins to smoke, gradually amp up the pressure and the speed until you're going pretty fast. You will notice the charred dust begin to collect in the carved notch. You can stop spinning when the dust starts smoking on its own. It is now a burning ember and will glow when you gently blow on it.

I've had embers burn as long as two minutes, so there's no need to rush to get the ember to your tinder. After the ember is formed and you've had a second or two to relax from spinning the spindle, gently remove your ember catch and carefully dump your ember in the middle of your tinder bundle and blow it into a flame.

YOUR SPONSOR HAS SENT YOU A

SURVIVAL QUICK TIP

I always place my ember into a small pile of dry-rotting punk wood (wood that is in the process of rotting; scoop this material out of old fallen trees or rotting stumps) inside of my tinder bundle. Sandwich your tinder bundle between two pieces of bark to protect your hands and keep them from getting burnt when you blow on the ember.

Don't expect to master the art of the bow drill on the first try. Even with expert instruction it takes trial and error to understand when and how to do certain things. But, I promise if you practice using the

Glowing ember

Blowing ember in tinder bundle into a flame

Credit-card-sized magnifying lens smoking a tinder bundle

Clear bag of water shaped to converge the sun's rays onto a tinder bundle

materials I mention in this book, you will be able to do it.

Magnifying Glass: Can a discarded glass bottle start an accidental forest fire? Yes, it can. Rays of sunlight can be magnified by a glass bottle and ignite flammable tinder on the forest floor. By design, a magnifying glass can converge the sun's rays to a super concentrated beam of light and heat that will ignite tinder. There are many items, such as the bottom of a glass bottle, that can do the trick. Other magnifying options include a camera lens, prescription glasses (far-sighted) and a binocular lens. Some of these items can be improvised from gear that you might have with you in a sudden survival scenario. Even ice and clear bags of water can be shaped in such a way to magnify sun rays. On a bright, sunny day, hold a lens at a dis-

tance above some fire tinder in a way that focuses the rays to the smallest focal point possible. The heat will be more intense as you position the lens to make a tighter focal point of light. If you've chosen your tinder wisely it will begin to smoke and smolder. If you're lucky, it will burst into flame. Or, you can place this ember into a tinder bundle and coax it into a flame by blowing on it, just like you do with an ember create by a bow drill.

MASTER FIRE BUILDING LIKE PEETA

Igniting flammable fire tinder is one thing, but building a fire and keeping it burning is a practiced skill in and of itself. The Hunger Games books don't specifically describe how Peeta builds his fires, but I imagine that it's very similar to my five-step fire building

Flat rock fire platform

Tree bark fire platform

Wood branch fire platform

method. You need to have each step of this process prepared and ready *before* you light your fire tinder. Time will be working against you and your only defense is proper preparation, especially when working with quick burning tinder material.

Step 1: Fire Platform

A good fire platform is a solid foundation for any successful fire, especially in damp, snowy, or wet environments. It will keep your dry tinder, kindling and initial flame off the ground. Even the slightest bit of moisture can affect your fire-starting material's willingness to burn. Your platform can be constructed from a huge variety of materials, both natural or man-made. I've used everything from flat rocks to a metal trash can lid. Three fire platform ideas are shown in the photos.

Step 2: Tinder Bundle and Ignition

After you build or choose your fire platform, igniting your fire tinder is the next step. For demonstration purposes, I am using a cube of WetFire in the photos. It is very important to have the next three phases of the fire building process prepared in *advance* before lighting your fire tinder.

Step 3: Toothpick Teepee

After your tinder bundle is burning, pile toothpick-sized twigs and splinters of wood in a teepee fashion around the burning tinder. Give these small twigs and splinters enough time to start burning.

Fire needs oxygen to burn. It may be helpful to fan and/or blow the small flame to help intensify the heat. It goes without saying that your fire kindling materials need to be as dry as possible.

Step 3: Toothpick teepee

Step 4: Q-Tip Teepee

Your next layer of fuel should be slightly larger than the first—around the size of a Q-tip. Stack these around the small fire in the same teepee arrangement. Allow them time to burn. Fan and blow as necessary.

Step 5: Pencil Teepee

As with before, your next layer of fuel should be larger—twigs about the diameter of a pencil. They should also be stacked like a teepee around the flame. Carving these into feather sticks will drastically improve your rate of success.

Step 4: Q-tip teepee

At this point, your fire should be steadily burning on it's own. You can continue to stack on larger limbs and branches. The key to this entire process is having all of your fire kindling collected before you ignite your fire tinder. There will be no time to run around and gather kindling while nurturing your small fire to life.

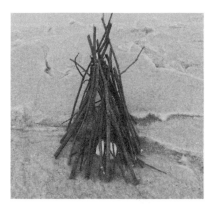

Pencil teepee with feather sticks

Teepee fire lay

Spit roasting squirrel

FOUR FIRE LAYS TO SURVIVE THE ARENA

Just as there are different shelter styles for different environments, there are different fire styles to suit different needs. These styles are called fire lays. Four distinct fire lays that would be helpful to tributes in arena are the

teepee, the long log, the log cabin, and the Dakota fire hole. Each lay has specific uses.

Teepee Fire Lay

The teepee fire lay is an all around multipurpose fire lay. It is the same style that I just described in the five-

Long log fire lay

Boiling water using tripod

Log cabin fire lay

step fire building method. I use the teepee as the starting fire for almost every fire I build. It is a great way to get some flames going.

Besides using it as a fire base, it is an excellent fire style for cooking small game or fish on a roasting spit. It works very well when cooking using a kettle and tripod as well. It is also a very effective warming fire in cold weather.

Long Log Fire Lay

The long log fire lay is specifically used for warmth in cold weather environments. A long, body-length fire is an exceptional way to keep warm in cold weather, especially when you are sleeping in an open-front lean-to shelter that can help to reflect the heat back down on you. This fire style also allows you to burn large logs that can be very difficult to use in other, more compact fire lays.

Log Cabin

The log cabin fire lay makes an excellent signal fire. I'll bet that this is the exact fire lay that Katniss and Rue build when luring the Careers away from the Cornucopia. When constructed properly, this fire lights and rages very quickly. After the walls are constructed, the inside is filled with flammable tinder and small pieces of kindling. I discuss how to use this fire lay to build a signal fire in chapter eight.

Dakota Fire Hole

Sometimes your survival depends on *not* being found. In the arena, a fire can give away your location and become a way for other tributes to track you down and kill you. If you are trying to hide and evade capture, but you still need a fire, the Dakota fire hole is a great fire lay option. Not only is it nearly invisible, but it also

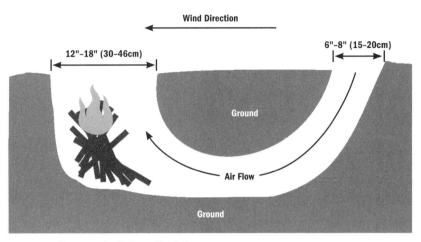

Wind Direction

12"–18" (30–46cm)

6"–8" (15–20cm)

Ground

Air Flow

Ground

Cross-cut diagram of a Dakota fire hole

burns efficiently and produces very little smoke. It is easy to cover up and leaves no trace. It isn't great for warming in cold weather, but it is excellent as a cooking fire. And, because your fire is basically built in an underground pit, it also performs very well in windy conditions.

The Dakota fire hole starts with two holes 18"–20" (45–51cm) apart and 12" (30cm) deep, as you can see in the illustration. Dig a tunnel roughly the length of your arm to connect the two holes. Build the fire in the larger hole; the smaller hole feeds the fire with air and oxygen. Ideally the

Dakota fire hole burning

Cooking over Dakota fire hole

holes are dug so that the wind direction crosses over the smaller "feeding" hole first. This design makes for an incredibly efficient fire that will burn very hot and smoke very little. Green sticks, a flat rock, or grill can be placed over the larger hole as a cooking surface. Don't cover the hole completely because airflow is critical to this design. If you don't have a shovel or digging trowel, I've found that a strong sharpened stick about the length of your forearm works as an improvised digging tool. Use it to break up the dirt and then scoop it out with your hands and repeat.

SUMMARY

The ability to catch fire in a real-life survival scenario is more important than I can't stress in words. Fire has a crazy number of practical uses to a tribute or anyone in a survival situation. I strongly urge you to practice the skills mentioned in this chapter in a responsible, safe, and controlled environment (with adult supervision if you're under eighteen). Whether you're in the arena or in a real-life survival situation, fire can be your No. 1 survival ally.

FIVE

TOOLS OF A SURVIVOR: KATNISS'S FORAGE BAG

WHETHER YOU'RE IN THE ARENA, foraging beyond the fence, or simply camping for the weekend, it's a good idea to keep a survival kit handy. While many survival tools can be improvised from natural materials, it can be very difficult and time consuming to make them. And, it requires a significant amount of experience and skill to do this.

Whenever Katniss heads into the woods, she first slings her forage bag over her shoulder. This bag is her personal survival kit and contains all the tools and items that she needs to hunt, prepare wild game, cook meals, set traps, and survive her excursions beyond the fence into the woods. Any outdoorsman or woman should follow her example.

Packing a forage bag like Katniss is a key survival lesson we can take away from the Hunger Games. We're never specifically told all the tools Katniss keeps in her forage bag, but

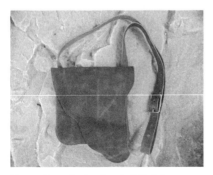

Forage bag similar to what Katniss might use

based on Katniss's activities in the wild, we can draw some very specific conclusions as to what items she carries. We will explore these items in this chapter so you can pack your own forage bag and practice the same survival techniques used by Katniss. We will discuss building a modern survival kit in chapter nine.

SURVIVAL KNIFE

A survival knife is one of your most important and most used pieces of kit. Follow Katniss's example and all the ways she uses her knife—to clean wild game, scale fish, build twitch-up snares, gather wild edibles, collect firewood, make roasting spits, and do all kinds of survival activities. Whenever you go beyond the fence, always carry a knife with you. In the arena, do all that you can (while still staying safe) to get a knife.

By definition, a survival knife must be able to perform in extreme conditions. Here's a short list of tasks a knife can assist you with:

- Cutting
- Hunting
- Dressing game
- Pounding/hammering shelter anchors
- Digging
- Self defense
- Splitting/chopping
- Making fire

Antler handle survival knife

Blackbird SK5 survival knife and sheath

Fixed blade knife and folding knife

- Carving
- Signal mirror (if blade is polished steel)
- Building shelter
- Food preparation

I wish I knew exactly what kind of knife Katniss uses. Maybe her dad made it for her using antler as a handle. Or maybe it is a relic handed down from the old world United States. I am left to wonder what it looked like and how it was styled. I do know that it must have been functional. If not, she would not have chosen it or continued to use it. Katniss is a very practical person.

You will probably use your survival knife more than any other piece of kit in your forage bag and choosing the right one is an important decision. Here are characteristics you should consider when choosing your survival knife.

Attributes of a Survival Knife

Fixed Blade: Your survival knife should have a fixed blade—not a folding-blade or lock-blade style. True, folding knifes can be more convenient to carry, but the strength of the knife is compromised at the folding joint. If the knife breaks during heavy use, you are in trouble. If you really like folding knives, carry one as a back up but not as your primary survival knife.

Full Tang: The phrase "full tang" means the metal knife blade and handle are made from one solid piece of metal. The metal handle is then sandwiched with knife scales to form a grip. The photo illustrates the difference between a full tang and what's called a rat-tail tang. Full tang construction is much more substantial and less likely to break during hard use.

Full tang blade (bottom) and rat-tail tang (top)

A full tang blade is much more robust and stable. It can withstand incredible abuse from demanding tasks, such as splitting wood—a task often called "batoning" in the survival community.

I own many non-full tang knives and love them all. However, they aren't my first choice in survival knife picks.

Sharp: Your survival knife should be razor sharp. It should shave the hair off your forearm. If it doesn't, buy a whet stone and hone the blade until it does. You should take pride in your knife's razor edge. A dull knife is more difficult and cumbersome to use effectively. You have to use more effort and more pressure (which leads to erratic carving and cutting) to perform tasks with a dull blade. A sharp knife is actually safer to use and is a more precise cutting tool that requires less energy and time as compared to using a dull knife. An accidental cut from a sharp knife is easier to dress than that from a dull knife as well.

Using survival knife to split wood (batoning)

Stabilizing knife with thumb while carving

Size Does Matter: As a rough estimate, the overall length of your knife should be in between 7" (18cm) and 11" (28cm). A knife that is much larger than 11" (28cm) isn't practical for delicate and detailed tasks. However, a knife smaller than 7" (18cm) is less capable of performing tasks that require a larger blade—especially demanding jobs.

Pointed Blade/Single Edge: Your knife needs to have a pointed blade tip. The point comes in handy for all kinds of chores. I broke the point off of my favorite survival knife and it drastically impacted the knife's effectiveness as a useful tool on many occasions. I eventually had to replace it.

Also, the knife blade should not be double-sided. Choose a single-edged blade only. You won't have a need for two sharp edges. The flat back ridge of a knife blade can actually serve several functions. Below are some of the most common:

- Striking a fire steel
- Used as a stabilizing platform for thumb or hand
- Pounding surface while splitting or batoning wood

HOW TO SHARPEN A KNIFE

I'm sure Katniss keeps a knife sharpening stone at home. Here's the simple step-by-step process I use to hone my knife blade each time I come back from the woods. You will need a knife sharpening stone (available in hardware and kitchen supply stores or online).

Step 1: Place your knife blade on the sharpening stone and make sure the angle of your knife's cutting edge is flush with the stone. Getting this angle right is very important. The angle of the cutting edge is different for every knife. As you can see by the diagram, this angle must rest flat against the stone as you sharpen. If the angle is too steep you will dull the blade, and if it is not steep enough the edge will not make contact with the stone.

Angle Grind of Blade

WRONG
Angle not correct

Sharpening stone

RIGHT
Angle correct

Sharpening stone

WRONG
Angle not correct

Sharpening stone

Two Kydex knife sheaths

Leather knife sheaths from Hedgehogleatherworks.com

I use the back ridge of my knife in these ways all of the time. A sharp, double-edged blade makes these important functions impossible.

Quality Sheath: A sheath is simply a case for your knife. There is nothing I hate more than a low-quality, poorly performing knife sheath. Many

Step 1

Step 2

Step 3

After a little practice you will be able to match this angle without thinking about it. You can buy a product called a sharpening guide to help you maintain the correct angle for your blade as you drag it across the stone.

Step 2: With slight pressure (about the same amount as if you were writing with a pencil) push the entire knife blade from point to heel across the stone (keep-ing the angle the same) almost as if you are carving the stone. (The point of the knife is its tip; the heel is where the blade ends against the handle.)

Step 3: Flip the blade over and at the same angle pull the entire knife blade back across the stone but this time from heel to point.

Step 4: Repeat this process eight to twelve times.

Knife made from flint rock

90-degree angle break starting point

Strike about a ½" (12mm) from the edge in a downward motion

knife enthusiasts feel the same way I do about quality sheaths. Poorly designed and cheaply made sheaths can be frustrating and dangerous to use.

A quality sheath should hold your knife in place snugly and securely. Your knife should not fall out when the sheath is shaken or turned upside down. At the same time, though, the knife should be easy to put in and take out of the sheath. You should be able to comfortably remove and insert the knife single-handed. Personally, I prefer molded Kydex or leather sheaths. Both are rugged materials that can handle extreme environments.

Even some great knives come with horrible sheaths. I've lost knives in the field due to poor sheath retention. A knife is an investment. If you find a great survival knife but hate the sheath, consider having a quality custom sheath made to match your knife.

Rue's Sharp Rock

In the arena (and unexpected survival situations), you aren't guaranteed access to a knife. Katniss gets her knife by luck, but you might not be so lucky. So what do you if you don't have a knife? Follow Rue's example and improvise. *Any* kind of cutting tool is better than *no* cutting tool at all! In Rue's case, she improvises a cutting blade from a sharp rock. I imagine that she uses that rock blade to gather wild edibles and prepare nuts and roots to eat. You'll need to do the same thing if you want to survive.

Our tribal ancestors survived for thousands of years using cutting tools made from sharp rock. In fact, rocks such as flint, chert and obsidian can be "knapped," or shaped, into useful blades that have razor-sharp cutting edges capable of carving wood, cleaning wild game, and making traps. Native Americans were masters of knapping usable blades and spear points out of flint.

Not all rocks are the same. Ideal rocks, such as flint and obsidian, are very fine-grained and will fracture in a pattern called a conchoidal fracture, which is perfect for nice sharp edges. Knapping a cutting blade, often called a "flake," from a piece of flint rock is easy to do. You simply need a piece of flint rock (or comparable stone) and another rock called a hammer stone. The hammer stone should have a solid striking end, like a hammer. I've used hammer stones of all shapes and sizes, but have found oval-shaped rocks about the size of a softball to be ideal. Before you start, you must break into the flint rock. Ideally you can create a 90-degree angle break through the rock.

As with any survival skill, knapping takes a little practice but is not

With a little luck, a flint flake will split off at your striking point

Continue this pattern until a sharp enough flake splits off to use for your purposes

Chip mark in flint rock that reveals the smooth flint inside

Grapevine lashed tripod

Grapevine lashed frame for debris hut

difficult to master. The most difficult part of this process is finding the right kind of rock! I've had the best luck in rocky creek beds. Many times the flint is hidden inside the rugged exterior of a rock that's been weathered for many years. The key is looking for little chip marks that reveal the nice clean fractures that are characteristic of flint and similar rock types.

Rock blades lack the durability of metal knives but can be incredibly effective cutting tools. If Rue can do it, you can, too!

CORDAGE

Cordage is a word used for any man-made or naturally gathered rope or cord. From gathering food to setting up shelter to securing equipment, the survival uses for cordage are plentiful. It will play an integral part in your forage bag. In chapter six, you'll learn how to use cordage to set up traps like Katniss and Gale use when they hunt.

You'll also learn valuable knot-tying skills. Knot tying is such an important survival skill that it earned its own station in the Hunger Games training hall. Every tribute needs to know how to tie strong, effective knots.

But you must have cordage before you can worry about tying it up. It's easy to carry cordage in your own personal forage bag survival kit, but it's also very important to know how to identify and improvise naturally occurring cordage options. You start with nothing in the arena (and many sudden disaster situations).

Vines

Creeping vines serve very well as quickly improvised cordage. I've never had much success with them for detailed knot work, but they work great for projects that don't require finesse. The vine I get most use from in the Eastern Woodlands is the grapevine. I prefer to use vines that are

Pine roots near ground surface

Pine root tied to hold shelter brace

around pencil-size in diameter. It also helps to soak the vine overnight in a stream or pond before use. I've found the vines become much more pliable after being soaked for a while.

Roots

Rootlets (small roots)—especially from pine and spruce trees—can make excellent cordage. Often, these roots will run just a few inches under the needle bed, and they can easily be pulled up. Sometimes you can even see them from the surface of the ground.

Rootlets are flexible and very tough. You can use them "as is" or they can be split into smaller strips for more detailed projects.

Inner Tree Bark

The inner bark fibers, just beneath the rough outer bark of many trees, is an excellent natural cordage option.

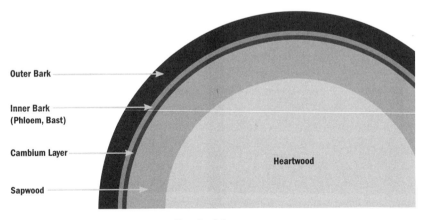

Outer Bark

Inner Bark
(Phloem, Bast)

Cambium Layer

Sapwood

Heartwood

Tree bark layers

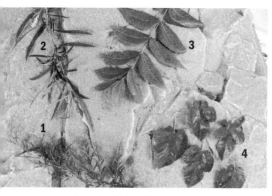

Tree Leaf Identification Diagram: 1.
Cedar; 2. Willow; 3. Walnut; 4. Mulberry

Inner bark fibers being stripped from a
cedar tree

Peeling inner bark from long-soaked
outer bark

My favorite trees for inner bark fibers are willow, cedar, mulberry, walnut, and slippery elm. Native Americans in the Pacific Northwest used cedar bark to make fishing line hundreds of feet long for hauling in huge fish. Inner bark fibers are incredibly strong, especially when reverse wrapped (shown later in this section).

The cedar is known for fibrous bark. To access the inner bark, make a cut through both the outer bark and the white inner bark, and then peel upward. Both layers will peel up in long strips. Then, the inner bark fibers can be separated from the outer bark with little effort. The inner bark doesn't easily peel away with many trees, such as walnut. I pulled the bark (outer + inner) from this walnut tree after a lightning strike shredded the tree. Soaking the bark in a nearby stream for two weeks made it very easy to peel off the inner bark in long, pliable strips. I coiled these strips up to dry for later use.

The bark from willow and mulberry saplings is very easy to peel up in spring and summer. It becomes more difficult to peel in winter months. I simply make a slice near the bottom and peel the outer and inner bark layers up as far as they will go. Then, I scrub off the outer bark by sawing the strips back and forth over a rough limb. Depending on the end use, it may not be necessary to remove the outer bark. You will always want to remove the outer bark when your are trying to make very fine cordage for items such as traps or fishing line. You can typically leave the bark on for less detailed chores.

Plant Fibers

Plants are my favorite source for natural cordage. Some plants have long fibers that run along the stem. It's these long fibers that make excellent cordage. If you're wondering how useful plant fibers can be, just look at all the ways Mags and Finnick use them in the Quarter Quell. They make shelters with woven grass mats and plaited bowls and containers. They have extensive knowledge of harvesting and working with plant fiber cordage. This section will give you this same knowledge, but its up to you to practice and build your skills.

My favorite three cordage plants are milkweed, dogbane, and stinging nettle. However, I've also harvested descent cordage from cattail, horseweed, burdock, and many grasses. The plant fibers of my favorite three are best harvested in the fall, after the first frost when the plant is dead and dry. At this stage, the hard, dry inner stalk can be broken and easily separated from the long fibers that run up

Dry coiled inner walnut bark

Peeling bark up from willow sapling

Scrubbing the outer bark by sawing across a rough limb

Dogbane plant

Milkweed plant

Separating dry stalk from fibers on the milkweed plant

Processed milkweed plant fibers

the outside. It helps to crush the entire stalk and then work up the plant in 2" (5cm) or 3" (8cm) increments. Once separated from the outer bark, any remaining plant pieces should be removed.

For milkweed, dogbane, and stinging nettle, it's easier, but not necessary, to harvest fibers from dead plants. Stinging nettle gets its name because it has thousands of stinging hair-like needles on its leaves and stalk. Because of these needles, it's best to wait until the plant dies after the first frost, or wear gloves if harvesting fibers from a live green plant. You can wipe the stinging hairs off with ease. I like to break off the plant near the base and then pull up the fibers and outer skin. They can be used

Stinging nettle plant

Pulling off skin and fibers from green stinging nettle

Green nettle fibers ready to use

Twisting the two ends of stinging nettle fibers to form a twisting kink in the middle

just like this with the outer skin still attached. I only use green cordage for temporary projects because it shrinks as it dries and this does affect the longevity of a lashing.

Reverse Wrapping Cordage

Many natural fibers don't hold up well on their own. Twisting them together using a process called the reverse wrap forms a much stronger and durable piece of usable cordage.

You can reverse wrap virtually anything—plastic, ribbons, and even strips of toilet paper (also known as prison rope).

Reverse wrapping is a series of well-placed twists that causes the rope to bind onto itself and hold the tight wrap. Watch a video of the process at

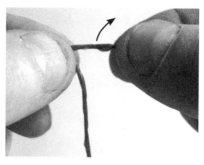

Step 1: Twisting upper fork away from you

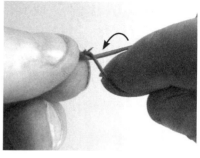

Step 2: Twisting the lower and upper forks one half turn back toward you

Rope developing with steps repeated

Twisting on more fibers to a short fork

willowhavenoutdoor.com/reverse-wrap-video. Here's a step-by-step description of how to do this.

Step 1: To start, select a piece of natural fiber. Hold one end in your left hand and the other end in your right hand.

Step 2: With your right hand, twist the fiber away from you. At the same time, use your left hand to twist the fiber toward you. Soon a kink will form in the middle and the fiber will begin to twist back on itself. Continue to turn your hands in opposite directions until the fiber kinks and three or

so twists form in the middle. Do not form this kink in the exact middle of the fibers; try to offset it to one side so you can splice in more fibers later on to make the rope longer.

Step 3: Now, hold the twisted kink in your left hand to keep it from unwrapping. The two loose ends will be pointing the same direction, one on top of the other. Your rope is starting to take shape. The kinked and twisted side is one end and the two loose ends (now facing the same direction) is the other end. The loose ends fork out of the twisted end so we will call them forks. With your right hand, twist the fibers in the top fork *away from you* one full twist.

Step 4: Pinch both forks and rotate them both one half twist back toward yourself so that the bottom fork is now on top.

Step 5: Repeat steps 3 (turning the top fork one full twist away) and 4 (rotating both ends a half twist back toward yourself) while keeping the developing twisted cord in your left hand to keep it from unraveling. You will begin to notice the rope taking shape, and tension from this twisting action will hold its form.

Eventually, you will run out of fibers in either the top or bottom fork. With about 2" (5cm) of fibers left, simply twist on a new length of fibers and continue twisting. This is why you offset the initial kink—so that both forks don't run out of fibers at the same time. If that happened, you would have to splice both ends in the same spot, which would create a weak spot in your rope. You can trim off the spliced tails later.

Cedar bark fibers reverse wrapped into a strong, usable cord

Reverse wrapped strips of toilet paper

CONTAINERS

From holding water to cooking food, containers play a valuable role in survival situations. Katniss probably carries a metal cook pot in her forage bag. Many of the wild greens and roots she loves so much are best prepared in a

Variety of metal cooking containers

Coal-burned container, step 1

Coal-burned container, step 2: Blowing coals using a reed-grass straw

metal pot. Besides cooking food, a metal container of some sort allows you to boil water. Boiling water is the only primitive water purification method I know of that is 100 percent effective. A metal container is a luxury to a survivor and should not be taken for granted. It can be very difficult and time consuming to improvise a suitable alternative from materials found in nature.

Plastic containers are also luxuries to survivors. They are water-tight and let you gather, store and purify water (chemically). Katniss is lucky to find a plastic container in the arena. You might not be that lucky. Natural containers are hard to find or make, but when you have no other options, you have to do the best with what you have. Here are some options for a naturally created container.

Coal-Burned Containers

One of the most durable natural containers I've ever made has been a coal-burned wooden container. You can use hot coals from a fire to burn a depression into a log, stump or large limb. It takes a little time, but this method is fairly easy and the hot coals do all the work.

Step 1: I like to start by carving out a small depression to hold the first few coals.

Step 2: Then, using a set of makeshift tongs (see chapter three for how to make these), place a few red-hot coals into the depression. Blowing the coals through a piece of reed-grass or bamboo intensifies the heat and helps to burn out the wood faster.

Step 3: Replace the coals as they burn and scrape out the inside of the depression every 10–15 minutes or so

Coal-burned container, step 3: Scraping out container

Finished coal-burned container holding water

using a knife, sharp rock, or shell. You can control the edges from burning by placing mud or wet sand on top.

Primitive civilizations have coal burned entire canoes using this exact same process. A container is a very small feat in comparison. And as I explained in chapter three, a coal-burned container is perfect for using hot rocks to boil water.

Earthen Containers

Native Americans were masters of using clay to make very impressive and durable containers. In much of the United States, clay can be found by digging a hole 2'-3' (1m) deep. The best place to find workable clay is along the edges of eroded riverbanks. As rivers erode their banks, clay becomes exposed and can be easily collected.

The easiest earthen container is a simple hole in the ground that is lined with clay. Simply build a fire in the hole to fire harden the clay for use as a temporary cooking pot or rock-boiling container.

You can also make a clay pot by coiling a "clay rope" base and then stacking clay coils on top to form

Fire hardened clay lined earthen hole vessel

Clay coil base

Clay coil sides

Smoothing sides with water

Bowl in fire

the container walls. After you finish the basic shape, use a little water to smooth both the inside and outside of the pot.

Let the clay pot dry in the open air for twenty-four hours. Then fire harden the pot to make it durable. To fire harden it, simply place the pot in a burning fire, surround it with wood and let the fire burn all the way down until the clay is cool to the touch. This may take overnight. The result will be a very usable piece of custom-made survival pottery.

Woven Containers

In the Quarter Quell, Mags is able to weave a water-tight grass container to hold sap that they extract from the jungle trees with a spile. Unless you devote your life to weaving, you won't be able to re-create a water-tight grass container. This type of craftsmanship is a true skill and takes many hours of practice to perfect. I would hate to be in a position where I needed to make a water-tight container out of grass. I'd be in trouble for sure.

Even thought they're not water-tight, woven containers can still be useful to you. Baskets woven from grapevine, willow, cattail, or palm leaves are fairly simple to make with little experience and are perfect for gathering wild edibles, such as nuts and berries.

Other Natural Containers

In the Quarter Quell, Katniss carries water back to camp in shells that she finds on the beach. This is an excellent use of natural improvised containers. While not large, freshwater mussel shells found in many waterways throughout the Eastern Woodlands make excellent small containers or cooking tools. You can also quickly craft a ladle for stews by chipping a hole in a mussel shell and then hafting on a wooded handle.

Ultimately, the lesson in survival containers is to keep a metal version in all of your survival kits. Nothing in nature even comes close to being as efficient and hassle free to a good old metal cook pot.

Woven container from palm leaf

Handmade willow basket

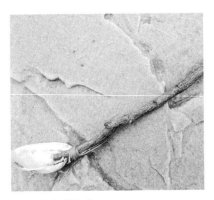

Mussel shell ladle

Sample survival fishing kit that Katniss might carry

Ferro rod and waterproof tin that contains dry tinder and char cloth

FISHING KIT

A fishing kit takes up virtually no space in your forage bag, and makes it much easier to catch some food. Katniss most certainly keeps a small fishing kit packed in her forage bag with supplies geared specifically toward bagging a few edible aquatic critters, such as fish, snakes, frogs, and turtles.

You can create a fishing kit that fits in your pocket. I keep my kit packed in a small aluminum pill case that I purchased at a local pharmacy. It includes:

- 30'–50' (9–15m) of 30-lb.+ test line
- 3–5 hooks in a variety of sizes
- 3–5 sinkers

You could also include a few cork bobbers and possibly even a steel fish/frog gig that can be quickly mounted to the end of long stick or cut sapling

for spearing anything within reach (we will discuss how to make your own fish gig in chapter six).

FIRE-STARTING TOOLS

If you've read chapter four, you already know how important fire is in a survival situation. With that said, it's vital that you keep fire-starting tools in your forage bag. You can be sure Katniss does. Her fire kit would most certainly include an ignition device and some dry fire tinder. Maybe a ferro rod with some naturally found tinder, or maybe a flint and steel with some char cloth. Cotton char cloth is an excellent fire tinder and has been used extensively by mountain men throughout history. I'll bet Katniss carries a tin canister that can be used to make fresh supplies of cotton char cloth when needed.

Making char cloth starts by placing pieces (usually 1" [25mm] squares) of 100 percent cotton cloth into a tin canister. This tin canister must have a small hole—about the diameter of a pencil lead—in the lid. Then, this canister is placed into a burning fire for just a few minutes. The heat from the fire will char the cotton cloth but not burn it. You will know it's ready when smoke stops shooting from the small hole in the lid. Char cloth will catch and smolder from even the smallest spark. Notice that you must have fire to make char cloth. Preparing and thinking ahead should be a part of your survival mentality. Be sure you understand the methodology of starting fires that we covered in the last chapter.

SUMMARY

We take many of the items in Katniss's forage bag for granted in our everyday lives. In nature, many of these vital items can be extremely

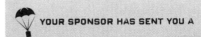

YOUR SPONSOR HAS SENT YOU A

SURVIVAL QUICK TIP

Make your own char cloth. Use a nail to punch a small hole in an empty and clean candy tin (like the tins Altoids mints come in). Cut a 100 percent cotton bandana into 1" (25mm) squares. Place three to five of these squares in the tin. Toss the tin in a fire for a few minutes and *voilà*, instant char cloth! Repeat the process for more char cloth.

difficult—if not impossible—to find or make. Do you have a forage bag that you take with you when venturing into the woods or traveling away from home? If not, it might be a good time to put one together or revise the one you already have to include some of the items Katniss carries.

SIX

BEYOND THE FENCE: SURVIVAL HUNTING & GATHERING

FOOD MAY BE PLENTIFUL in the Capitol, but in the outer districts, diets are limited and people often go hungry. If you're brave (or desperate) enough, you can join Gale and Katniss as they venture illegally beyond the fence to gather wild edible plants and hunt game. The game you catch can feed your family or be traded for other necessities, such as medicines, salt, and paraffin. When possible, follow Katniss's and Gale's example by partnering with at least one other person to combine your strengths. Working in a team is a very important part of the survivor mentality.

If you're ever in the arena or a real-life wilderness survival situation, you'll have a huge advantage if you can forage food from nature. While you can survive up to three weeks without food, it would be a miserable three weeks and you would be too weak to do much of anything by the end of the first week. You need food to keep up your strength and help you survive. Katniss aces her wild edible plant test at the Training Center. Could you? This chapter will teach you how to hunt and trap small animals and identify edible plants growing wild (in the real world). Keep in mind, Katniss's hunting and gathering skills didn't come easy to her. Her skills are based on many, many hours of practice, trial, and error, as well as training from her father. If you want to be as good as she is, you'll need to practice, too.

CREEK'S THREE RULES OF WILD EDIBLE PLANTS

Katniss tells us that District 12 was once known as Appalachia. It's coal-mining country, likely the area we call West Virginia, which is in the Eastern Woodlands. Eastern Woodlands is a broad geographic term used to describe all of the U.S. states located between the Atlantic Ocean and the Mississippi River. All of the plants that I discuss in this chapter can be found in the Eastern Woodlands. I live in this region and I am intimately familiar with all of the wild edibles Katniss encounters during her trips beyond the fence and into the woods. Before we get into the specifics of those edible plants, I want to issue my three rules for gathering wild edibles.

Rule 1: If in doubt, leave it out. This simply means that if you are not 100 percent certain of a plant's identity beyond the shadow of doubt, then leave it be. The consequences to eating the wrong wild edible can be severe and even fatal. Don't leave anything to chance. Heed the words of the edible plants training instructor when he tells Katniss not to eat any berries unless she is 100 percent sure they aren't toxic. I wholeheartedly agree with this philosophy. Mother Nature can be a very tricky Gamemaker. In many instances, there are poisonous look-alikes to edible plants.

Rule 2: Focus on the 20 percent of plants that you see 80 percent of the time. There are hundreds of wild edible plants out there. I don't even come close to knowing them all. When it comes to wild edible plants, I keep it pretty simple. I focus on the ones that are readily available—the ones I see all of the time—not the ones that require significant effort to locate or that have poisonous look-alikes.

I also focus on the plants that have significant food value and that are fairly easy to prepare. For example, there are many plants that are edible but are so small they'll do little to fill you up or provide you with energy, and so they have no significant food value. I skip these plants. I also skip plants that are difficult to harvest or prepare. If a plant requires three or four changes of boiling water to eat, I don't waste my time. This rule alone will help keep you focused when searching for and harvesting wild edibles. Your efforts are best spent on certain plants. Just because it's edible doesn't mean it's worth your effort.

Rule 3: Get a good field guide. Katniss's mother and father had started writing a book identifying wild medicinal and edible plants—

their version of a present-day field guide. Even with years of experience in gathering and eating wild edibles, I almost always reference one or two field guides when foraging. The one I use most often is *A Field Guide to Edible Wild Plants: Eastern and Central North America* by Lee Allen Peterson. For further study of the plants mentioned in this chapter, as well as many others, I suggest picking up a copy of that field guide.

WILD EDIBLE PLANTS OF DISTRICT 12: THE EASTERN WOODLANDS

Go to www.livingreadyonline.com/hungergamesedibles to download a free, full-color guide to the wild edible plants mentioned in this chapter.

Dandelion

While most people view dandelions as annoying weeds, Katniss sees them as a valuable, life-giving source of food. They will keep her family from starving to death as long as they are in bloom. The dandelion is an amazing wild edible. It is easy to identify and to my knowledge has no poisonous look-alikes. I regularly eat every part of the dandelion. It is tasty and very easy to prepare. It also grows almost everywhere. The entire plant is edible from bloom to root—minus the fluffy seed pods when the blooms mature. The seed pods might be edible as well,

Dandelion

Boiled dandelion root with a little butter

but I've never tried to (or wanted to) eat them. The green dandelion leaves grow in a basal rosette very close to the ground. The leaves are deeply toothed and are lance-shaped. Dandelions are easiest to identify by their bright yellow sunburst flower that appear in early spring—though they are edible year-round. When I was a boy, I always associated this yellow flower with a lion's mane to remember the name dandelion. Dandelions also have a white milky sap if you break the leaves or flower stalk. This sap is the source of the sometimes bitter flavor dandelions have.

Dandelion roots can be cooked like root vegetables (carrots or potatoes, for example), and the leaves can be cooked like spinach as a pot herb or added raw to salads. Cooking the leaves removes the slightly bitter flavor. The young tender leaves are best for salads. In fact, an expensive or-

ganic market near my home sells dandelion leaves for an outrageous price. I always laugh at that. I've also eaten the blooms raw. They are better when batter-fried in a wash of egg, milk, cornmeal, salt and pepper. My mom prepared this dish all the time as I was growing up in Southern Indiana. This is still one of my favorite foods. You can eat the dandelions growing in your own yard (or any other yard), as long as the yard hasn't been treated with chemical fertilizers, pesticides, or herbicides.

Visit willowhavenoutdoor.com/dandelion to view detailed color photos of dandelions.

Wild Onion

I've always considered wild onion an ingredient rather than a stand-alone food. I'll often add a bit of wild onion to a salad or on a fire-roasted rabbit to enhance the flavor. The green tops

Wild onion bulbs

Pokeweed

can be used just as you would chives, and the underground bulbs make perfect additions to stews or chopped up and cooked with other root vegetables. In fact, the green, spiky wild onion tops look exactly like chives that you would see in the supermarket. They are typically about the size of pick-up sticks and grow in very noticeable "bunches." You will know these by their very "oniony" smell once you break open the green leaves.

Wild onions grow best in wide open sunny spaces and show up in very early spring. They thrive along treelines and fence-rows and do very well in wasteland type environments.

Visit willowhavenoutdoor.com/wild-onion to view detailed color photos of wild onion.

Pokeweed

Pokeweed is another plant I grew up with, gathering with my mom. I was eating poke long before I knew that most people didn't eat it. Pokeweed is a little tricky. It's fairly easy to identify and only the young shoots 12" (30cm) or less should be harvested. The mature leaves, stalks, and berries (purple when mature) are all poisonous. The root is also poisonous. The stalk begins to turn a purplish shade with age. Ignore anything with any shade of purple. Other than that, poke is an excellent potherb and I especially like it mixed in with scrambled eggs. It can also be added to soups and stews.

Poke has large oval-shaped leaves that are a vibrant green. I can spot poke amidst other vegetation from many feet away because of its uniquely colored leaf. It stands out in a crowd. Poke thrives in semi-shaded areas along forest edges. It pops up in early spring and then matures into large purple stalked plants that I've

Pokeweed berries (poisonous)

Pine tree

seen grow as tall as 8' (2m). Often, there will be small poke plants growing around larger mature plants.

Visit willowhavenoutdoor.com/pokeweed to view detailed color photos of pokeweed.

Pine Tree

Katniss tells us she's eaten plenty of pine and it is one of the foods she eats in the arena. Aside from the needles, I've never been a big fan of the edible pine tree. I make pine needle tea every chance I get. Simply boil a handful of pine needles in a mug of water to make a very nutritious tea packed with vitamin C. I've heard that one cup of pine needle tea can contain as much as five times your daily requirements of vitamin C, making it a super survival beverage. If you are boiling water for purification, you might as well toss in some pine needles while you are at it.

I've eaten the inner pine bark before, but can't imagine eating much of it. To me, it tasted like cardboard that had been marinated in Pine-Sol cleaning solution. It just wasn't my

 YOUR SPONSOR HAS SENT YOU A

SURVIVAL QUICK TIP

Scurvy is a disease that occurs when you don't get enough vitamin C. In winter survival scenarios where fresh fruits, greens, and vegetables are scarce, you'll find enough vitamin C in pine needles and rose to prevent the onset of scurvy. Symptoms of scurvy include swollen gums, skin lesions, depression, fever, and loss of teeth. Without treatment (adding vitamin C to the diet), scurvy is fatal.

Pine needle tea

Inner pine bark

Katniss plant (arrowhead plant)

thing. But in truly desperate food situations, it will fill you up and keep you going. The inner pine bark isn't difficult to access. Simply scrape or peel off the rough, gray outer bark and you'll find the edible inner bark layer just beneath. If you are lucky, you can peel the inner bark off in strips, or you can do like Katniss and just scrape off handfuls of the stuff. I've had it raw and I've also had it sun-dried like a pine chip of sorts. I preferred the dried chips.

I *love* pine nuts. Let me rephrase that. I love pine nuts when I can buy them in a big package at the store. Harvesting pine nuts from pinecones is a very tedious task. It's best done by placing the mature but unopened pinecone near a fire. The heat from the fire causes the pinecone to open up, and then the nuts can be picked out. It takes a lot of pine nuts to make any kind of difference to an aching belly, but they are a nice addition to a fresh salad or roasted trout.

Visit willowhavenoutdoor.com/pine to view detailed color photos of pine trees.

Katniss Plant

Did you know Katniss got her name from a wild edible plant? That's right, the katniss plant, which is also known as the arrowhead plant. It is an aquatic plant that grows in marshy areas or at the edges of water. It has an edible tuber that is best harvested in the fall and is prepared exactly like you would a potato. It was a staple wild edible food in the diet of Native Americans.

The katniss plant is easily identified by its arrowhead-shaped leaves. I think it's pretty cool that Katniss is named after an arrow-shaped plant and just happens to be an expert markswoman with the bow and arrow. The green arrowhead-shaped leaves of the katniss plant can grow quite large. A telltale identifying indicator of the katniss plant are the veins along the back side of the leaf. Notice how they look like a spider—branching out like spider legs from a central point.

Visit willowhavenoutdoor.com/katnissplant to view detailed color photos of the katniss plant.

Katniss tubers will float when they are dislodged from the mucky mud in which they grow. Many Native Americans harvested the tubers by stomping through the water where the Katniss plants grew. This stomping would work the tubers loose from the mud. Once loose, the buoyant tubers could be easily gathered as they floated to the top of the water.

Cattail

Speaking of aquatic plants, the cattail is probably my favorite wild edible plant. It has edible parts all year long.

Arrowhead plant tubers

Veins on backside of katniss plant leaf

Green (edible) cattail seed head (pollen forming section on top)

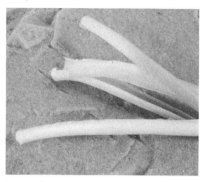

Heart of cattail

"Asparagus-like" cattail rhizome

In the spring, while the seed head is still green, it can be boiled and eaten just like a mini corn on the cob. Don't expect a corn flavor, though; it's 100 percent cattail. When the seed head starts to turn brown, it's no longer good to eat.

The yellow pollen that forms on the top section of the seed head is also edible, but in a short-term survival situation, it isn't worth your effort unless maybe you wanted to add some to a stew or soup as a thickener. To collect the pollen, tie off the arm and head holes on a T-shirt and shake the pollen into the shirt. Otherwise, it is very difficult to collect and blows away quickly in even the slightest breeze.

I also enjoy the inner stalk of new cattail shoots that are less than 24" (61cm) tall. The stalks can be eaten raw, but when I eat them uncooked, they make my throat feel a little scratchy, so I prefer to cook them like a stir fry vegetable or as an addition to stew. Just peel away the outer leaf layers to reveal the white inner core that is edible. You can pull these stalks right out of the plant in the ground. Grab the inner-most section of the plant around 6"–8" (15–20cm) from the bottom and firmly pull up. The center stalk will pull right out. Then, peel away the outer sheath of leaves to reveal the edible nonfibrous middle portion.

My favorite edible part of the cattail is the new rhizomes, or underground stems. In the spring, cattail plants send out new horizontal rhizomes that eventually turn up and become new cattail plants. If you catch them at the right time, you can just snap off the creamy white pointed rhizome shoot. They are delicious when prepared like asparagus.

Visit willowhavenoutdoor.com/cattail to view detailed color photos of cattail plants.

Jerusalem artichoke plant

Jerusalem artichoke tubers

Jerusalem Artichoke

This plant is not an artichoke, and I don't think it comes from Jerusalem, either. The name is actually very odd considering this plant belongs to the sunflower family and has a small sunflower bloom in late summer. The edible part is the starchy tuber, which should be gathered in the winter after the first frost. You can cook these exactly like potatoes. These plants spread like crazy and come up year after year. They need lots of sun and are most often found in wasteland type environments and fields. I plant them along the forest edge at Willow Haven and consider them a backup survival garden. The tubers will keep all winter in the ground and you can dig them up as needed. I've seen Jerusalem artichoke tubers for sale in high-end organic food stores under the name sunchoke. If you want your own crop, buy some tubers at the store and plant them just like you

would plant potatoes. Or, you can just find some in the wild.

Jerusalem artichoke plants grow very tall. They have a coarse, hairy stalk and pointed lance-shaped leaves that alternate in position up the stalk. These features, combined with the yellow flower bloom in late summer, make this plant fairly easy to identify.

Visit willowhavenoutdoor.com/jerusalemartichoke to view detailed color photos of this plant.

Stinging Nettle

This is an amazing wild edible from a very unlikely candidate. Stinging nettle greens is one of my favorite wild edible dishes. You can cook the young plants and new leaves at the top of the older plants like you would spinach. As they grow older, just pinch off the top 2"–3" (5–8cm) because the rest of the plant becomes quite bitter and fibrous. Be careful as you harvest this plant. The tiny hairs along the stem

Stinging nettle plant

Tiny stinging hairs along stem

pack quite the itchy punch if you brush them on your skin. Cooking the plant neutralizes this toxin, so don't worry about getting an itchy tongue. And yes, this is also the same stinging nettle that we discussed in the cordage section of chapter five.

The leaves of stinging nettles are very toothed—like a saw. They grow opposite each other along the stalk. Nettles very much resemble wild mint (mentioned later), except without the minty flavor. When I'm in the mood for stinging nettle soup, I look for these plants in moist, wooded areas down by a creek or in a shady area. Many times, though, stinging nettle will find you *before* you find it.

 YOUR SPONSOR HAS SENT YOU A

SURVIVAL QUICK TIP

Stung by the stinging nettle? No worries—Mother Nature provides a remedy typically within a stone's throw. Rub on the juice from the stems of jewelweed and it will instantly relieve the stinging itch from the stinging nettle. See detailed photos of jewelweed at willowhavenoutdoor.com/jewelweed.

Jewelweed, a stinging nettle remedy

It just takes one sweep across the arm to know you are standing in a patch of stinging nettle plants.

Visit willowhavenoutdoor.com/stinging-nettle to view detailed color photos of this plant.

Cooking stinging nettle greens in a small cook-pot

Lamb's-quarter

I make a mean lamb's-quarter soup with cattail pollen, milk, wild onions, salt and pepper. Lamb's-quarter can be added to soups and stews and can also be cooked alone as a potherb like spinach. It is an excellent wild green and is best gathered when the plant is young. It is very easy to identify with its leaves having a white powdery underbelly. Lamb's-quarter has a very pleasant mild flavor and the young tender leaves make excellent additions to fresh salads. You probably have lamb's-quarter growing in your backyard and don't even know it. Once you learn how to identify it, you'll see it all over the place. This wild green is at the top of my favorites list. I have no doubt that when Katniss gathers wild greens, lamb's-quarter is among them.

Lamb's-quarter plant

A slang name for this plant is goosefoot because the diamond-shaped, softly toothed leaf slightly resembles a goose's foot. They grow very tall in maturity (up to 6' [2m]) and branch out like crazy. I eat the leaves from this plant from early

Wild mint

Wild mint tea

Curly dock

Handful of mature dock seeds

spring until late fall. You can find it almost anywhere. It loves wasteland environments, like old construction sites, barren roadsides, and field edges. It is almost always one of the first plants to pop up in disturbed soil.

Visit willowhavenoutdoor.com/lambs-quarter to view detailed color photos of this plant.

Mint

Wild mint has two distinct identifying features: a strong minty smell produced when the leaves and stem are crushed, and its square stem. I rarely find wild mint, but when I do, there is a lot of it in one spot. Katniss is fond of mint and often adds it to other foods for flavor, and even chewed on the leaves to ease hunger pangs. You can do the same.

Mint isn't really a standalone food but is best added to other dishes; it is especially good with meats, such as rabbit and quail. Mint also makes an excellent tea. Simply boil six to ten mint leaves in a cup of water for a few minutes for one of the best wild teas that you can make.

Wild mint likes moist areas; I've only found it along rivers and streams. The jagged toothed leaves grow opposite each other along the square, hollow stem. Always identify mint by crushing the leaves to reveal its distinctive minty aroma.

YOUR SPONSOR HAS SENT YOU A

SURVIVAL QUICK TIP

A sharpened digging stick that is 2"-3" (5-8cm) in diameter and approximately 24" (61cm) long is perfect for digging up wild roots. It can also function as an impromptu throwing weapon if you jump some wild game.

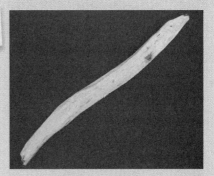

Creek's digging/throwing stick

Visit willowhavenoutdoor.com/wild-mint to view detailed color photos of this plant.

Curly Dock

I imagine Katniss often gathered curly dock in the wild. Young dock leaves have a sour, tangy flavor that I actually like. The leaves can be eaten raw when they are young, but are best boiled in one change of water after they mature. It makes an excellent spinach-like dish.

Curly dock leaves have curly and wrinkled edges—hence the name. The lance-shaped leaves grow quite long. I've seen some as long as 18″ (46cm). They are very easy to spot amongst the other grasses and weeds in early spring. They show up primarily in very sunny, open areas. I don't think I've ever seen a dock plant in the woods. As the plant matures, it produces a center flower stalk that is topped with hundreds of small seeds.

The seeds are also edible and can be ground into flour or boiled in water and eaten as gruel similar to oatmeal or grits. If you boil the seeds, add some berries or honey if you have them to make the dish far more enjoyable to eat.

Visit willowhavenoutdoor.com/curly-dock to view detailed color photos of this plant.

Wild Edible Plants Summary

Entire books have been written on identifying wild edible plants. As I mentioned in my three rules of wild edibles, I highly recommend you get a good, comprehensive wild edibles field guide, such as *A Field Guide to Edible Wild Plants: Eastern and*

Arm covered in nice, sticky mud

Camouflaged hand with mud and forest debris

Central North America. The wild edibles I've listed in this chapter are some of my favorites (and probably some of Katniss's favorites, too). All of them fit my wild edible plant criteria of being easy to find, easy to identify and easy to prepare. None of them will disappoint.

Download a free quicksheet reference guide that includes fast facts and color photos of all the wild edible plants discussed in this chapter online at www.livingreadyonline.com/hungergamesedibles.

HUNTING, TRAPPING, AND FISHING IN DISTRICT 12: THE EASTERN WOODLANDS

In the wild, it's impossible to survive long-term on edible plants alone (especially in certain climates and seasons). You will need the additional calories found in meat and fish to survive. Katniss's trapping, fishing, and archery skills all combine to make her an excellent small game hunter. Whether it's rabbit, squirrel, groosling, or fresh fish, Katniss is always on the hunt for meat. She knows how important meat is to her survival. This section details some hunting, trapping, and fishing strategies that you can use to put meat on the table.

One thing I really like about Katniss is that she doesn't rush into anything. She takes the important steps necessary to help ensure a successful hunt. Three of these important steps include *camouflage, tracking* and *stalking.*

Camouflage

Forest animals are acutely aware of their surroundings. They live by survival instinct. There is no better camouflage in a forest environment than real forest debris. Even the most expensive camouflage hunting clothing and gear cannot perfectly mimic actual sticks, leaves, mud, and weeds.

Peeta draws on his artistic background to effectively camouflage himself, but you don't need an artistic background to apply this principle during your own hunt. Here are the steps I take when I use natural camouflage:

Step 1: Get dirty! A base layer of mud is critical in natural camouflage. First, it provides a muted earth-tone background color. Second, it provides a sticky surface that will keep forest debris on your skin.

Step 2: Decorate! Next, while the mud is still moist, stick on as much forest debris as you can. This includes dead leaves, green leaves, bark pieces, and whatever else is naturally around your chosen hiding spot. If you are camouflaging your entire body, it

YOUR SPONSOR HAS SENT YOU A

SURVIVAL QUICK TIP

It's all about the *smalls*—the little critters like fish, frogs, snakes, crayfish, crabs, rabbits, lizards, squirrels, mice, rats, rodents, bats, birds, turtles, possum, and raccoons. It's easy to get caught up in the idea of a big game hunt with some fancy fashioned hunting set, but at the end of the day, it just isn't all that practical. Your survival will depend on your ability to hunt, kill, and eat the *smalls*.

might be easier to just roll around on the forest floor after you have a good base layer of mud. When the mud dries it will glue the leaves and forest debris in place.

Animal burrow

Animal game trail in snow

Rabbit droppings

Several small game tracks along trail

Game trail along stream edge

You can also touch up areas with cooled charcoal from a fire. Katniss uses this camouflage method in the arena to disguise her orange backpack. Charcoal also works great as camo face paint!

Tracking

Katniss is always on the look out for signs of animal activity. Whether searching for water or on a small game hunt, Katniss uses animal clues to guide her steps. Animal signs are especially important when setting twitch-up snares, which we will discuss later. Obviously, being able to track animals in the forest can be an advantage when hunting them. There are several telltale signs of animal activity. These include scat (droppings), tracks, rubs, scratches, signs of feeding, shelter or burrow entrances, food and water sources, and well-traveled game trails.

These game trails, called "runs," typically lead from the nest, shelter, or den to water and food sources. Animals are the ultimate survivors and also live by the survival code of energy conservation. Consequently, several animals may travel the same trail or path on a regular basis. Animals travel the path of least resistance, and hunting or trapping along these regularly traveled runs will increase your chances of success.

Stalking

Stalking is an important part of hunting because you typically have to surprise an animal to be able to catch it. Stalking skill takes practice. You'll likely start out like Peeta, who is clumsy and loud—snapping sticks and crunching leaves. All this noise alerts animals to danger and sends them running away. But with lots of practice, you can become like Gale, who is very quiet and graceful when traveling through the woods.

Every step you take on the forest floor should be calculated and purposeful, almost like a choreographed dance with the trees, rocks, leaves, logs and earth. It helps to stay on the balls of your feet while inspecting each spot you want to place your foot before you take your next step. Stalking is slow and methodical and requires a great deal of patience.

One With the Forest

You'll know the moment when you get the steps of camouflage, tracking, and stalking right. The forest will come alive around you as you hear the animals go about their daily routines completely unaware of your presence. It is truly an amazing moment when you experience this for the first time. You will become one with the forest. Now, you are ready to hunt.

KATNISS AND GALE'S HUNTING & TRAPPING TOOLS
Twitch-Up Snare

Gale's famous twitch-up snares—Katniss thinks so highly of them that she gives Gale a bow and arrow in exchange for teaching her how to make and set these snares. And she's right; these snares are a great way to catch small game, like rabbits, without expending a lot of time and energy. This is a must-have survival skill for the arena and real-life wilderness situations.

Time and energy conservation are both very important factors to consider in any survival situation. This is precisely why snares are such important survival tools. After you construct and set a snare, you can focus on other survival priorities while

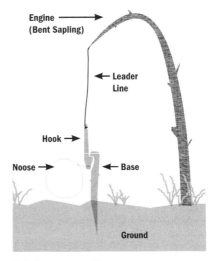

Twitch-up snare diagram

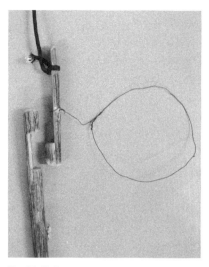

Real twitch-up snare

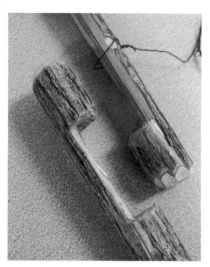

Close-up of carved hook and base

the snare keeps working. Snares will keep working even while you are sleeping. With ten snares, you can hunt in ten different locations at the same time while expending *zero* energy. You become a one-man hunting party. Snares are a survivor's secret weapon. Not only are snares incredibly reliable and effective, they also require very few resources (materials, energy, and time) to build.

Before you even think about spending time and energy on building and setting a snare, you must first determine which animal you want to target with your snare. For survival purposes, small game represents your best chance of success. While the twitch-up snare can be scaled up to catch animals as large as deer, it is more practical to target small game

animals, such as rabbit, squirrel, and ground-dwelling fowl, such as quail or grouse. This snare can also be modified to fish for you as well. Not only are smaller game animals easier to catch and field dress, but you can set numerous small game snares using the same amount of time and materials it would cost you to set one larger snare. Setting snares is a numbers game. The more snares you set, the greater your odds of success. This is why Katniss always sets multiple snares.

The twitch-up snare can be effective in virtually any climate and any environment on any continent. It can be deployed any time of the year and is equally effective day and night. From desert to rain forest, I can't think of a place where you can't use some version of this snare to catch small game. With that said, placing random snares throughout the woods is foolish and a waste of time and energy. Though they can be baited to draw in animals, snares are most effective when strategically placed in-line with existing small game trails like we discussed earlier.

The snare's trigger consists of two parts: the *hook* and the *base*. As you can see in the diagram, the *leader line* is tied to the top of the hook and the *noose* is tied to the bottom of the hook. The *engine* (typically a bent over sapling) provides tension to the hook, which is secured under the base—until an animal disengages the hook by pulling on the noose. The leader line from the hook to the engine can be any type of cordage. The line needs to be strong enough to withstand the initial "spring jerk" and then the weight of the suspended (and struggling) animal.

The hook and the base can be carved from two branches about the diameter of your thumb. I've included a close-up photograph so that you can visualize how you need to carve them.

You can also quickly improvise a hook and base from two Y-branches. I've provided a close-up photograph of this as well. You will need to cut them so that the smaller hook catches on the larger base. This method doesn't require carving, only locat-

YOUR SPONSOR HAS SENT YOU A

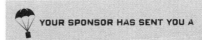

SURVIVAL QUICK TIP

When carving your hook and base trigger system, do not use *green* wood. The sap from green branches will nearly glue the two triggers together and make them more difficult to dislodge. Use only dead, dry, solid branches.

ing two Y-branches that will suit your needs and cutting them accordingly.

Thin wire is the best material to use for the noose portion of the snare. Katniss uses the coil of wire she found in her orange survival pack inside the arena. I'm certain she also keeps snare wire in her forage bag, as well, for setting snares beyond the fence at District 12. Here's how to make a noose:

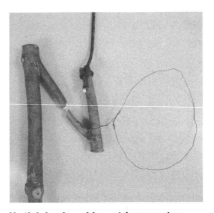

Y-stick hook and base trigger system

Step 1: Create a small loop about the diameter of a pencil on one end of the wire. Bend over the end and wrap the wire back onto itself three or four times to secure the loop.

Step 2: Next, thread the other end of the wire through the loop you've just created to form a noose.

Step 3: Secure the free end to the bottom of the hook trigger by wrapping it around the hook and then twisting the wire back onto itself three or four times, similar to how you made the loop in step 1. When using wire for your noose, no knots are used—only twisting.

The size of the noose depends on the size of game you are trying to snare. For rabbits and squirrel, a noose of 6"–8" (15–20cm) in diameter is sufficient. The noose must be large enough to accommodate your target's head and then about 20 percent larger to increase your chances of success.

As long as it will hold the struggling weight of your target animal, the leader line can be almost any kind of cordage. I tie the leader line to both the hook and the engine with a knot called the double half hitch, also known as two half hitches. I've provided a photo to illustrate how to tie this binding hitch knot. I have also filmed a video demonstrating how to tie this knot at willowhavenoutdoor. com/double-half-hitch.

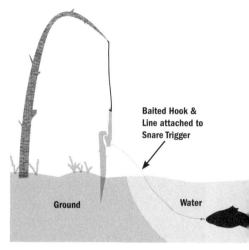

Baited Hook & Line attached to Snare Trigger

Ground · Water

Twitch-up snare modified for fishing

This same trigger snare principle can be used with a hook and line for fishing as well. Instead of using a noose, attach your fishing line to the bottom of the hook trigger using a standard fishing hook knot. When a fish pulls your line and disengages the trigger, the engine will pull and

Double half hitch illustration

set the hook in the fish's mouth. Make sure your trigger hook is just barely set so that the slightest tug from a nibbling fish engages the engine. I have also filmed a video demonstrating how to tie a standard fishing hook knot at willowhavenoutdoor.com/fishing-hook-knot.

Fish Spear/Gig

Katniss mentions spearing fish on several occasions. I prefer to call this "gigging." When I think of a spear, I think of a large throwing spear for hunting big game like boar. It's fairly easy to make a primitive fish gig that is also perfectly suited for gigging other small game animals such as frogs and snakes. A fish gig is a great hunting tool to have on hand and can serve as a walking staff as well. Here's how to make a small-game hunting gig:

Step 1: Find a sapling that is between 6'–8' (2m) long and about 1" (3cm) in diameter and trim all the branches off it. I love using willow saplings for gigs, and they typically grow near water anyway.

Step 2: Use a knife or sharp rock to split the thicker end of the sapling. Split down the middle of the shaft about 10" (25cm).

Step 3: Turn your knife perpendicular to your first split so it forms a cross in the center of the shaft, and make a second split as deep as the first.

Maple sapling for fish gig

Split and spread gig tip

Sharpened and lashed fish gig

Stand of willow tree saplings

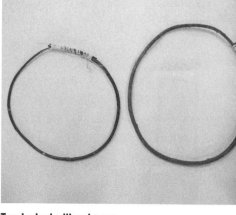

Two lashed willow hoops

Step 4: Find two small sticks. Wedge one at the bottom of the first split. Then wedge the other stick at the bottom of the second split so they make a cross. These small sticks spread the end of the sapling into four prongs.

Step 5: Sharpen each of the four prongs to a fine point.

Step 6: Strip the bark from the sapling to create bark cordage and use it to lash the base of the split. Lashing the base of the split prevents it from splitting further. You don't need to lash the gig if you'll be using it for only a short time, but if you think you'll use the gig for a while, it will hold up better if you lash it.

Using your camouflage and stalking skills, use your gig to spear or pin small game, such as fish and frogs.

Gale's Fish Trap

Gale is an expert at making fish traps and nets. With a little effort, you too can make a primitive fish trap similar to what Gale would have made. It's called a funnel trap, and it can be made from a small grove (thirty or so) of willow saplings that are ¼"–½" (6–12mm) in diameter. Conveniently, willow almost always grows near water. Here's how to make the funnel trap:

Step 1: Cut about thirty willow saplings between ¼"–½" (6–12mm) in diameter. Trim all the branches from them.

Step 2: Strip the bark from the saplings. The bark will be used as the cordage for weaving and keeping the trap together.

Step 3: Select two saplings. Bend each to form two separate hoops. One

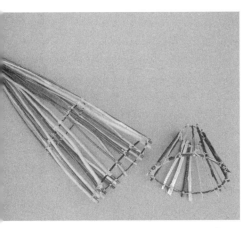

Trap body with lashed on willow shafts

Cone tied in place with bark strips

hoop should be approximately three-quarters the diameter of the other. In the example in the photo, one hoop is 12" (30cm) and the other is 8" (20cm). Use the bark cordage to lash the ends together and secure the hoops. The size of the hoops will determine the size of fish you can catch—the larger the hoops, the larger the fish.

Step 4: Create the body of the trap by lashing a series of willow shafts approximately 1" (25mm) apart along the outside of the hoops. In this example, the willow shafts are approximately 4' (122cm) long. Trim the shafts as necessary as shown in the photo. The ends of the willow shafts at the tapered end should be tied together. The fish will enter the trap from the open end.

Step 5: Select two more saplings. Bend each to form two sepa-

rate hoops. One hoop needs to be the same diameter as the largest hoop you made in step 3 (12" [30cm] in this case). The second hoop needs to be half the size of the first hoop (6" [15cm] in this case).

Step 6: Lash a series of willow shafts that are approximately 10"–12" (25–30cm) long about 1" (25mm) apart along the outside of the hoops to create a cone that does not have a tapered top. This cone is the cap (entrance) of the trap. This small funnel will direct fish into the trap but make it very difficult for them to exit in the opposite direction.

Step 7: Place the cap in the body of the trap, as if you were stacking them with both small ends pointing the same direction. Line up the body and the cap so the hoops that are the same size are touching. Lash these

Bait

↓

Gorge in Bait

↓

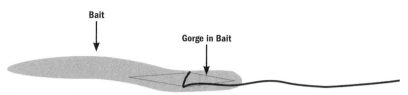

Baited gorge diagram

hoops together with bark. With this configuration, fish can swim into the trap but are unable to find their way back out.

Step 8: Hang your bait from a bark strip in the center of the trap.

Place the trap in an area where you've sighted fish. Tie it off to a tree or root so it doesn't float away and check it every few hours. You can increase the size of your trap by increasing the diameter of the willow hoops you create and the length of the sapling "ribs."

Making Primitive Fishhooks Like Mags

Mags, being from a coastal district, has some serious fishhook-making skills. You can join her ranks with these three primitive fishhook designs.

Primitive Hook #1: Gorge. A gorge isn't actually a hook at all. The name is an indicator of function. A gorge is something the fish actually eats, and when baited properly, the gorge catches in a fish's throat, preventing the fish from slipping off the fishing line. A gorge must be baited in paral-

Primitive fish gorge made from bone

Wild Rose Bush Thorns

lel with the fishing line so that when the line is tugged the gorge pivots and catches in the fish's throat or mouth. See the baiting diagram for a visual explanation.

A gorge can be made from a thorn, a carved piece of wood, a little piece of metal, or a carved piece of bone. I've had the best success with bone. One scavenged piece of bone can yield many fishing gorges. Carve your chosen material so that both ends have very sharp points that will catch in the fish's throat.

Primitive Hook #2: Thorn. Thorns make excellent fishing hooks. They aren't great for large fish or for long-term use but are capable of bringing in small fish and bluegill. I've made hooks with thorns from both locust tree and wild rose bushes.

Locust tree thorns

The hardest part of fishing with primitive gear is getting your hook tied on your line so it's sturdy and stays in place. When you're looking for thorns to use as hooks, it's important to choose a thorn that has another thorn or nub along the stem to act as a stopper for your fishing line. I've taken several close-up photos of thorn hooks I've gathered to aid in your selection process.

Primitive Hook #3: Lashed Hook. The lashed hook design is the most time-consuming of the three hooks I've mentioned. To make it, you have to carve two pieces of wood or bone and lash them together. Here's how to make a lashed hook:

Step 1: Select a piece of wood about the diameter of pencil. If it's a long piece, cut it into two pieces, making one piece half the length of the other.

Locust thorn hook tied with an inner strand of paracord

Rose thorn double hook woven into natural cordage

Step 2: Cut one end of the longer piece so it is at a sharp 70-degree angle. Whittle the shaft of this piece toward this point so the other end is thicker and will catch the line to keep it from slipping off.

Step 3: Whittle the shorter piece so it is the same diameter as the shaft of the long piece. Then cut one end to a 70-degree angle that will match the angle on the long piece. These two pieces should fit together, as the picture shows.

Step 4: Cut the other end of the short piece to a 40-degree angle the opposite direction of the bottom angle (as the photo shows).

Step 5: Line up the two pieces so the matching angles touch and wrap and lash the bottom portion so that they stay together. I'll often soak my cordage with pinesap, which will stiffen after a while and help hold the

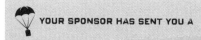

YOUR SPONSOR HAS SENT YOU A

SURVIVAL QUICK TIP

Live meat stays *fresh*! If possible, keep wild game alive until you are ready to eat it. You can string fish through the mouth and gill on a length of natural cordage and leave them in the water with the cordage tied to something on shore until you are ready to eat.

lashing. You can also make a natural pine resin glue by heating pinesap and mixing it with crushed charcoal from your fire pit. To make this glue, I use three parts pine resin to one part charcoal. It's delicate work, but the end result is a fairly solid hook. Notice the node at the top, which helps to hold

Lashed hook, step 4

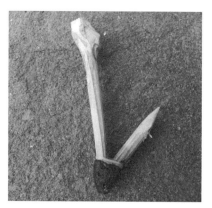

Carved and lashed hook with pine resin glue

Splitting off a third of the sapling

Notched tip

the line in place. For this example, I used cordage fibers from stinging nettle to lash the bottom of the hook and then dabbed on a little pine resin glue.

Make an Improvised Survival Bow

In a real-life survival situation, I'm typically not a big fan of spending the time and energy required to make elaborate improvised hunting tools. But, Katniss makes great use of a bow and arrow both outside and inside the arena, so I can't leave out this option. (Katniss would be very disappointed in me.)

Let me begin by stating that archery is a *skill*. If you can't shoot a bow and arrow *now*, then don't expect to be able to shoot one in a sudden survival scenario. If archery is a skill you want, you'll need to get the proper equipment, seek out quality instruction, and practice, practice,

practice. After you have this skill set in your arsenal, making a quickie survival bow might be a viable hunting tool for you. Here's the simplest way I know of to make a quick, effective survival bow.

The Bow

Step 1: Find a sapling about 1"–1½" (3–4cm) in diameter. For a short-term bow almost any type of wood will work. Good options are hickory, maple and osage orange. The sapling must be straight and free of burls, kinks or weird deformities. Also, select one with few branches. Ideally, the main bow section will be 4'–5' (1.5m) in length.

Step 2: Split away approximately a third of the bow to make it more flexible. The easiest way to do this is to drive your knife (called "batoning") down the entire length of the

Timber hitch knot, step 1

Timber hitch knot, step 2

Timber hitch knot, step 3

bow. The side with the bark still on it is the side that faces *away* from you when you hold the bow.

Step 3: After you've made your initial split, shave off more wood from the inside (split side or side without bark) of the bow to reduce draw weight if the bow is still too difficult to bend. There is no need to remove the bark or carve a handle. The arrows will rest directly on your hand.

Step 4: Carve simple notches on both ends of the bow to secure a bowstring. Hopefully, you have some viable man-made cordage with you to use as a string. If not, you'll have to make a bowstring from natural options, which is going to be very time-consuming in a survival situation. Use a timber hitch knot on the bottom end of the bow and secure the top of the bowstring using two half hitch knots (detailed previously).

I've included a photo of a timber hitch on the notched bow tip. This should be enough to illustrate exactly how to tie this knot, but you can also view a video demonstration online at willowhavenoutdoor.com/timber-hitch.

The Arrows

The best arrows are made from seasoned, dried wood. However, in an impromptu situation, this isn't always possible. Dried cattail stalks or

Split tip bamboo, sharpened mullein and locust thorn tipped cattail arrow points

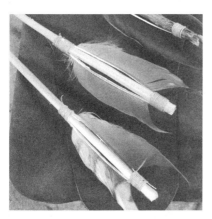

Improvised feather fletchings and bow string nock in each arrow

In a survival situation, yours won't be the only hungry belly you need to worry about. Animals will be attracted to any food you prepare or eat in the wild. Protect yourself and your food by doing the following:

- Always field dress wild game at least 200 yards (180m) from your camp. The smell of blood and entrails can draw in predators that might consider you a meal.

- Place any leftover food in a container or bag and hang it from a high branch at least 100 yards (91m) from where you camp to keep out scavenger animals.

- Properly and thoroughly clean your cooking utensils to keep them sanitary and remove the smell of food. Pinecones, horsetail, sand, snow, and reindeer moss all make excellent natural pot scrubbers.

mullein stalks that are still standing from the previous year make excellent short-term arrow shafts. They are typically pretty straight and very light weight. The points can be sharpened or split to make fishing or bird arrows. Thorn, bone, or sharp rock arrow points can also be lashed in place for a more deadly strike. Bamboo and river cane also make excellent arrows.

For fletchings (the feathered part of the arrow that helps it fly with more accuracy), scavenge feathers,

Quickie survival bow and arrows

split them, and lash them to the shaft using natural cordage. You must carve notches at the butt end of each arrow to provide a secure seat for the bowstring. (These notches are called nocks.)

If your arrow shafts are bowed or slightly crooked, heat them over a fire and flex them to a straight position until cool. They typically hold their new shape after this process.

AFTER THE HUNT

So, what happens if you're lucky enough to bag some wild game with a hunting tool or trap? You now have to field dress it and cook it. Katniss is no stranger to cleaning and preparing wild game on the move with just

her knife and an open fire. These are important survival skills. Here are a few basic Katniss-style wild game-cooking techniques that can easily be used in a survival situation.

How to Make a Roasting Spit

When it comes to roasting game over an open fire, a few tips can make this process a whole lot easier. There is an art to making a roasting spit.

You will need two solid Y-shaped sticks to act as supports for your spit stick. Sharpen the bottoms of these sticks so that they can be hammered into the ground.

The spit stick that holds the game needs to be a branch cut from a fresh, green, nonpoisonous tree, such

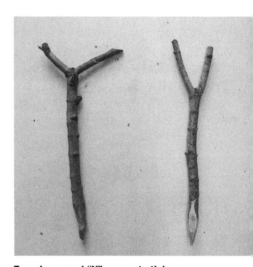

Two sharpened "Y" support sticks

as maple, oak, hickory, or sassafras. Notice the details in the photo of my sample spit stick. I cut a stick that has several branches on both ends and also has a couple sticks in the middle. Take your time and search for a branch that has these same features. This style of branch is very important because it lets you skewer your game on the little branches in the middle so the game doesn't spin while the stick is rotated over the fire. If your spit stick has these mini-skewers, you won't need cord or wire to hold your game in place. The branches on the ends allow you to place positioning stakes in the ground on each side, which can hold the spit in place exactly where you want it. This frees you

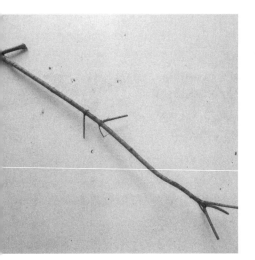

Green roasting spit stick

Squirrel on spit over fire (notice how the mini skewers hold it in place)

Cooking stew over two logs

Cooking stew over two rocks

Cooking stew with a pot and tripod

to do other things while your food cooks instead of constantly baby-sitting the cooking spit.

The Art of Stew

Making a stew is pretty basic. Throw some meat, vegetables, and seasoning in a pot with water, bring it to a boil and then let it simmer to cook. From what Katniss describes, Greasy Sae is a master of the stew pot. There are three methods to cooking stew over an open fire.

If your pot has a handle, the first method you can use is to hang your pot from a tripod. This is the method I prefer because the tripod allows you to easily lower or raise the stew pot to control the cooking temperature.

The second method is to place two larger rocks (roughly the same height) on either side of your fire (your fire will need to be narrow) and balance your stew pot between both rocks so the fire is beneath the post.

The third method is the same as the second except you use two small logs to support a stew pot for cooking. This is an old mountain man trick.

SUMMARY

There is a ton of information in this chapter. Nature is loaded with food options if you know how and where to look. A well-rounded knowledge

YOUR SPONSOR HAS SENT YOU A

SURVIVAL QUICK TIP

If you take an animal's life for food, be sure to use *all* of the animal. An animal has many uses to a survivor besides just meat. The entrails and other scraps can be used as bait for snares and traps. Primitive cultures also used the twisted intestines of many animals to make very strong bowstrings. Bones can be used for tools, weapons, sewing needles, fish-hooks, and even snare triggers. The animal hide can be used to make clothing, containers for rock boiling, arrow quivers, forage bags, and even glue. Animal hide (leather) also makes very durable and useful cordage. To get the most cordage from any size hide, cut the hide in a spiral pattern starting from the inside and work your way to the outside. Many feet of cordage can be cut from even a very small hide if you use this technique.

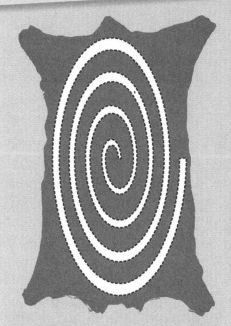

Cutting hide in a spiral pattern to make cordage

of wild plant edibles, hunting tools, and trapping techniques can be life-saving information to a survivor.

Download the quicksheet reference guide of all the edible plants discussed in this chapter and take it out on your next foraging adventure. Go to www.livingreadyonline.com/hungergamesedibles.

SEVEN

SURVIVAL FIRST AID: HEALING BASICS FROM KATNISS'S MOM

IN MODERN SOCIETY, we take healthcare and first aid for granted. In large cities like The Capitol, doctors are only a few minutes away and there are pharmacies on nearly every street corner. In an emergency, an ambulance staffed by trained medics can whisk you away to the nearest hospital where specialists can treat you with the best equipment and medicines.

First aid in remote wilderness areas like District 12 or the arena is quite a different story. Suddenly, you must rely on your own knowledge of first aid and medicine to treat unexpected injuries and illness. When you have limited access to medical supplies and facilities, even simple injuries and accidents have the potential to be deadly.

In a survival situation, your health is one of your greatest assets. Your health directly impacts your strength, stamina, and mind-set. This chapter will teach you the basics of first aid in the wilderness, following the principles used by Prim and Katniss's mom. For this chapter we ask the question WWKMD—What Would Katniss's Mom Do?

KNIFE CUTS, SPEAR SLICES, AND FLESH WOUNDS

Cuts, scrapes, punctures, and lacerations are not uncommon wounds in a survival scenario. We all know the arena is a deadly place. Hand-to-hand combat with knives, spears and other weapons is a given. It's unlikely a tribute will survive a fight without some kind of injury that breaks the skin, whether it's a stab wound, a cut, or some other kind of flesh wound. In a disaster situation, falling or flying debris can cause injuries. In a wilderness survival situation, a fall or even improper knife handling can cause a flesh wound.

Severe flesh wounds often require modern medicine to fully heal, but in a wilderness situation, it may be a while before you can get access to medicine (or it may not be available at all). Still, there's a lot you can do to treat knife cuts, spear slices, and flesh wounds in a wilderness environment.

General Treatment
Step 1: Thoroughly clean any type of flesh wounds with purified water and

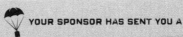

YOUR SPONSOR HAS SENT YOU A

SURVIVAL QUICK TIP

Willow bark contains salicin, which is similar to acetylsalicylic acid (aspirin). Chew on green willow twigs to help relieve headaches and minor discomforts.

Oak acorns

Dandelion leaf poultice

Mullein plants

a mild soap to help prevent infection. Irrigate the wound with plenty of purified water to remove any debris or dirt. Anything left in the wound can cause an infection and an infection can lead to a fever, gangrene, and, if severe enough, even death. Using purified water is important—you don't want to introduce bacteria to your bloodstream through contaminated water. If you have access to an antibiotic cream, apply it to the wound.

Step 2: Cover the cleaned wound with a clean, dry dressing, or bandage. If no first aid supplies are available, cut clean clothing or fabric into strips and use them as bandages. Boil dirty fabric to sterilize if necessary and then thoroughly dry before using.

Step 3: Routinely check the dressing and change it as needed, or at least once a day. Keep the dressing as dry as possible.

Natural Remedies

Antibacterial cream can be hard to come by in the wilderness and in the arena, but there are several natural remedies you can make that are antiseptic or antibacterial.

Oak Acorns: You can make an antiseptic wash for a wound by boiling oak acorns. The tannic acid in the acorn will leech into the water, making it a mild antiseptic. Boiling will also disinfect dirty water. Rinse the acorns and prefilter the water before you boil everything together. This will keep the wash free from debris.

Dandelion: Dandelion is known to have some antibacterial properties as well. The fresh juice squeezed from dandelion leaves can be applied to minor scrapes and wounds to help prevent bacterial infections. A poultice can also be made from the crushed leaves (simply crush the leaves in your cook pot and apply to the wound).

Close-up mullein leaf

Mullein Plant: You may not have access to proper bandages or even extra clean clothing and fabric. If this is the case, the large fuzzy leaves from the mullein plant make excellent impromptu natural bandages and are also said to be mildly antimicrobial. Rinse them with purified water to remove any debris and let them dry before you apply them. You can use natural cordage to hold the leaves in place.

Improvised mullein leaf bandage

Blisters

Even a small blister can be a huge setback to a traveling survivor. When your feet are in trouble, you are in trouble. Once a blister forms, it can be very difficult to treat. The best strategy is prevention. Wool hiking socks, such as SmartWool brand, provide excellent padding and also help to wick moisture away from your

Moleskin

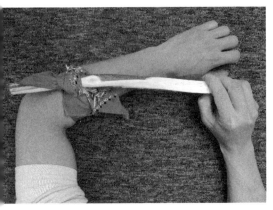

Winding bandana tourniquet

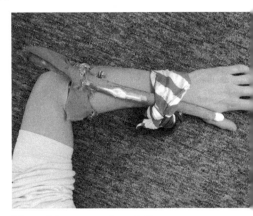

Tying stick to prevent unwinding

feet. They are also much less likely to bunch and shift. In addition to good socks, always carry moleskin patches in your first aid kit. Promptly cover any developing "hot-spots" with a moleskin patch to prevent a blister from forming. I've also used the soft green leaves from the Mullein plant as a natural Moleskin. Mullein leaves aren't as durable as moleskin but will work in a pinch.

TOURNIQUETS

Deep wounds are serious and can require extra first aid attention. If you cannot control blood loss with bandages or direct pressure, a tourniquet may be your only option if the wound is on one of your limbs. (Tourniquets can't be used on your trunk.) Katniss's mother shows her how to make and use a tourniquet and this knowledge serves her well in the arena. Using

a tourniquet is a first aid skill you should learn, too.

A tourniquet cuts off blood flow to any part of the body that is below it. A tourniquet should be a last resort and should be released every few minutes to allow blood flow to the arm or leg. Tissue that doesn't have blood flow will die and gangrene will set in. Here's how to use a tourniquet:

Step 1: Your tourniquet should be made from fabric that is 2"–4" (5–10cm) wide. A bandana or shirt sleeve is the perfect candidate. Do not use a thin cord or wire!

Step 2: Wrap the tourniquet about 3" (8cm) above the wound (towards the body) but below the nearest joint if possible. Tie it in place with an overhand knot. Place a stout stick, pipe, or bar across the knot and tie another overhand knot on top of it. Now, twist the tourniquet until the pressure stops the flow of blood. A second piece of fabric can be used to tie this stick in place and prevent it from unwinding.

Step 3: Every few minutes, unwind the tourniquet enough to allow blood flow to return.

FIRE BOMBS, FLAME-THROWERS, AND BURNS

Disasters destroy gas lines, down power lines, and expose flammable materials to volatile conditions—so you'll likely encounter some sort of uncontrolled fire in a disaster survival situation. And you never know what kind of tricks the Gamemakers will play in the arena. Just look at what happens to Katniss. Whether caused by flames, chemicals, heat, or radiation, many burns are treated the same way.

General Treatment

Step 1: Similar to a cut or scrape, the first step is to gently wash the burn with purified water. It's also important to treat the burn with cool water for fifteen to twenty minutes.

Step 2: Remove anything, such as loose clothing, that may irritate the burn.

Step 3: Apply an antibiotic burn cream (if available) and loosely wrap the burn in a clean gauze dressing or other clean fabric. Regularly check the dressings and change them daily. If blisters form, leave them alone. They will heal more quickly if left undisturbed.

Natural Remedies

Aloe Vera: The aloe vera plant is a very popular natural burn treatment and is an ingredient in many name-brand, over-the-counter sunburn ointments. Break off a leaf from the plant and squeeze the gel in the leaf onto your burn. It's very unlikely you'll find aloe vera growing wild in the Eastern Woodlands, but it is a common ornamental houseplant.

Cattail: The gel in between the leaves at the base of cattail plants can also be used to soothe mild burns. Apply this gel as you do aloe vera gel.

Aloe vera plant

YOUR SPONSOR HAS SENT YOU A

SURVIVAL QUICK TIP

To remove a tick, firmly grasp the tick as close to your skin as possible using tweezers from your first aid kit. Do not grab the tick by its body. Doing so can force fluids from the tick back into your skin, which can lead to infection. Pull outward in a firm, steady motion. Twisting or jerking motions can break off parts of the tick's mouth and head in your skin, which can also lead to infection. After the tick is removed, wash the affected area with soap and water. When walking through wooded areas or high grass, wear long pants and long sleeved shirts to help keep ticks off your body.

VIPER BITES AND TRACKER JACKER STINGS

The smallest little critters can completely ruin your day in the woods. Some insect and snakebites can be downright deadly without access to modern medicine. We're fortunate that we don't have to worry about tracker jackers outside of the arena, but there are plenty of stinging and biting animals that can cause you serious harm. Even the sting from a common honey bee can be deadly to someone who is allergic. Avoiding poisonous insects and snakes is the best policy. Do this by watching where you step. Listen and look for hives (especially ground hives) before you climb or disturb a tree; especially a rotting one, or one that is hollow inside.

Snakes rarely bite humans without provocation and warning. Know the poisonous snakes in your area so you can identify one if you see it. Poisonous snakes in the Eastern Woodlands are copperheads, timber rattlesnakes, and cottonmouths (also known as water moccasins; they live near water primarily in southern states). If you encounter a poisonous snake, stay calm and slowly move in the opposite direction and give the snake space to make its own retreat.

Trust me, it wants to be away from you more than you want to be away from it.

To best avoid being bitten by a poisonous snake, follow these four guidelines:

Step 1: Treat *all* snakes as *venomous*. Keep your distance from any snake—regardless of whether or not you think it is nonpoisonous. The presence of *any* snake is an indicator that there may be other snakes in the area. As tempting as it may be, don't go in for a closer look.

Step 2: If you are in geographic areas known for poisonous snakes, try to avoid places where snakes like to hang out, if you can. This includes high grass, scrub brush, creek and river banks, and wooded areas. Travel by roads or trails if these are available. Snakes are masters at camouflage, and the best way to avoid them is to travel a path that is clear and free of grass and forest debris.

Step 3: If possible, always wear boots and long pants. If a snake does strike, solid boots and long pants have a much better chance of deflecting venomous fangs than sandals and shorts.

Step 4: Watch where you step! When traveling in the outdoors, you can easily become careless. These are the most dangerous moments. If you are in snake territory, do your best to inspect the trail ahead of you to avoid surprising a resting snake. Remember, snakes want to avoid you if possible. They will only strike when provoked or surprised. Try not to surprise them.

If you are bitten, do your best to specifically identify what bit you so you can properly treat the wound and eventually relay that information to medical professionals, if possible.

If you are allergic to any kind of sting or bite, carry an EpiPen with you at all times.

Treatment for Poisonous Bites

If you've been bitten by a deadly poisonous snake or are suffering from an allergic reaction, I'm afraid there isn't

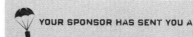

YOUR SPONSOR HAS SENT YOU A

SURVIVAL QUICK TIP

Wild animals should be leery of humans. Beware of any wild animal that appears to be slow, approachable, or tame. This may be an indication of injury, sickness, or even rabies. Never attempt to capture, kill, pet, or eat a wild animal that exhibits unnatural or odd behavior. It isn't worth the risk. Prevention is the most effective treatment.

Plantain plant

Plantain leaf bandage holding poultice on finger

Squeezing gel from jewelweed stalk

much that can be done without access to modern medicine and treatment. The best first aid treatment is to keep calm, stay hydrated, and lie down. If you're in a group, send someone from your party for help and stay put. An injection of epinephrine can ease the effects of anaphylaxis (allergic reaction) if an EpiPen is available. Do *not* attempt to suck the venom from the bite. This is a popular treatment in movies and novels, but in the real world it's not helpful and can actually cause more damage.

Treatment for Nonpoisonous Bites

Less lethal stings and bites from bees, mosquitoes, spiders and ticks should be washed with soap and purified water and then treated with an antibiotic ointment if available.

Natural Remedies

A bug bite may not be lethal, but it can certainly be painful, itchy, or irritating. Inside the arena, Rue chews up leaves to make a very effective ointment for tracker jacker stings. It seems to almost instantly relieve inflammation and swelling. There is a weed in your backyard that has a very similar medicinal use.

Plantain Plant: The plantain plant was used by Native Americans to treat a huge variety of ailments, earning it the nickname of the Band-Aid plant.

It has both anti-inflammatory and antiseptic properties. You can make a poultice by mashing and grinding the leaves with a little warm water (or chewing them in your mouth like Rue) and applying this paste to swollen stings or bites. The plant's antiseptic properties will also help prevent infection. The mature leaves are very fibrous, and you can tie them around wounds to hold a poultice in place if necessary.

Jewelweed: Also known as the spotted touch-me-not, this plant has a long history in helping to soothe skin irritated by poison ivy, stinging nettles, and insect bites. The oily gel that can be squeezed out of the stems gives almost immediate relief to stinging nettle. This is an excellent plant to use for a variety of skin inflammations and irritations, including itchy bug bites.

SUMMARY

Wilderness first aid is a vast subject with entire books dedicated to it. If you ever find yourself in a remote wilderness environment or a disaster scenario with limited access to modern medical supplies and facilities, make a mental and physical effort to be extra cautious. Don't take unnecessary risks and always think before you act. Prevention is the absolute best first aid policy I can recommend.

If you'd like to explore wilderness first aid in more detail, I recommend you take the Wilderness and Remote First Aid course offered by the American Red Cross. More information can be found at www.redcross.org.

YOUR SPONSOR HAS SENT YOU A

SURVIVAL QUICK TIP

Plantain has both external and internal healing properties. Not only can it be used as a poultice to treat stings and bites but you can also make Plantain Leaf Tea to help sooth coughs and break up mucus in the lungs. To make plantain tea, add four or five plantain leaves to a cup of boiling water and let it steep for ten minutes. Strain out the leaves and drink.

EIGHT

NAVIGATING THE CAPITOL: TIPS AND TRICKS FOR TRAVEL, RESCUE, AND EVASION

SURVIVING THE ARENA requires both physical and mental skills. Navigation and signaling are two mental skills that will greatly improve your odds of survival in both the arena and real-life emergency scenarios. The Hunger Games are often a waiting game. If you can effectively evade the other tributes, you might make it to the top five or six before you are forced into hand-to-hand combat. But staying out of the way means being constantly on the move. You'll need good navigation skills to help you return to water and food sources and the Cornucopia, and to avoid enemy camps. You can't afford to wander aimlessly around the arena.

In real-life survival situations, you'll need navigation skills to find your way out of danger or back to civilization. Signaling skills will help you communicate with search and rescue teams that are looking for you and help you communicate with anyone you are traveling with.

Katniss finds herself in numerous situations where she has to use her knowledge of nature, navigation, and signaling to increase her odds of survival. You might not be so lucky to have a Holo holographic map to help you navigate through peril. The skills discussed in this chapter can help you navigate in and out of a survival scenario, whether you are attempting to self-rescue or signal a rescue crew.

STAY PUT IF POSSIBLE

If you ever find yourself in a real-life survival scenario, your best option typically is to stay where you are and wait for rescue. Get yourself to the most visible area in sight (an open field, hilltop, etc.), and stay there. Let the search and rescue crews come to you. A sitting target is easier and faster to find than a moving target. Move only if it is more dangerous to stay than to leave.

DETERMINING A DIRECTION OF TRAVEL

North, south, east, west—what do these four words mean to a lost survivor? Not much if you don't know where you are or where you are going. However, if you know what direction you came from (for example, your plane was traveling east when it ran out of gas and had to land in the forest), then you know which direction home is—west. The ability to accurately determine direction then becomes very important.

Sometimes, it's most important to consistently travel in the *same* direction, regardless of which direction that is. In varied terrain or dense forest, it's easy to walk in circles if you don't know the direction you are heading or if you don't stick to one direction. To consistently travel in one direction, you *must* be able to figure out at least one of the four cardinal directions—north, south, east, or west. If you can determine one, then you will know the other three. Without being able to accurately determine direction, it can be very difficult to travel in a straight line. Choosing a direction and traveling in a straight line toward that heading is critical. Eventually, if you travel in a straight line you will cross some kind of road, waterway, fence, or path that you can then follow to civilization.

As I said in the sidebar, in many real-life survival scenarios, it is best to stay where you are and wait for rescue. If your situation requires you to travel, make your best guess as to which way to go and then continue in that same direction until you find a waterway or a sign of civilization. The topics below can't help you choose your direction but they can help you *stay* on it.

ORIENTEERING

Tributes don't receive maps of the arena, and the Gamemakers change the layout, landscape, and climate

---

DEFINITIONS

Cardinal Direction: A primary direction used for navigation. There are four cardinal directions—north, south, east, and west. Remember the layout of a compass rose by envisioning the directions on the face of a clock. If north is noon, east is three, south is six, and west is nine.

Heading: Your direction of travel.

Orienteering: The skill of using a map and compass to navigate across unfamiliar territory.

---

each year (and sometimes even during the games), so orienteering will be of no help there. However, Katniss uses a Holo holographic map to help her outside of the arena. And in real-life survival situations, orienteering can be a lifesaving skill. Always pack a map of the area you are traveling and a compass in your forage bag or backpack anytime you go out in the wild, even if you plan to stay on well-marked trails in a state or national park. This is part of being properly prepared.

If you are completely lost, a map and compass are going to be of limited help. However, depending on the circumstances, it is possible to use a map and compass to put enough pieces of the puzzle together to make an educated guess for travel.

Compass

Obviously, a compass is used to determine direction. With the help of a compass, it's fairly easy to travel in a consistent direction. But a word of caution is needed: Compasses are driven by the Earth's magnetic pull and metal objects near or around your compass can cause it to give you an inaccurate reading. Make sure you are not around metal objects when taking a compass reading.

Area Map

Again, if you don't know where you are, a map of the area will be of limited value. Landmarks, such as rivers, streams, lakes, roads, or mountains, can provide clues as to your location even if you are completely lost. For example, in the simple diagram that follows, if you are lost and you know you were headed east but haven't crossed the river yet, then you can at least determine your general whereabouts by continuing east until you reach the river. Referencing and comparing the landmarks you see *on the map* and the landmarks you see *in real life* can help you determine your location.

In this hypothetical situation, after you reach the river, you can follow

A few sample compasses

Compass reading due north

Metal survival knife next to the same compass which now reads NW

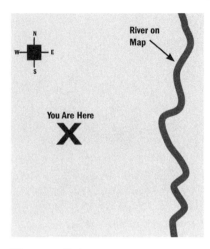

River map diagram

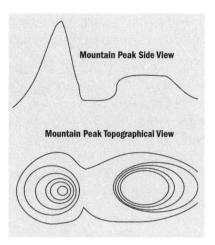

Topographical map

it downstream until you find another recognizable landmark on your map. At that point, you can determine exactly which way you need to travel to reach another destination that you've chosen on the map.

Topographical Maps

Topographical maps have lines that indicate elevation. Closer lines indicate steeper elevation. See the diagram in which I have notated a steep hill and a flat plain based upon the topographical lines. This is very basic way of visualizing a map in 3-D.

It is possible to determine your location by analyzing the topographic lines on a map and then studying the landscape around you. Identifying extreme landscape features, such as mountain peaks, can help you figure out your general location in reference

to those peaks on a topographical map. It's tricky but possible.

It is very easy to imagine that you could be lost or stranded without a map or compass. If you are, there are a few natural navigation tips you need to learn.

NATURAL NAVIGATION

In the arena, it's up to you alone to figure out the lay of the land. There are no maps, and it's very unlikely you'll have a compass. You'll need to follow Katniss's example and let nature be your guide. Whether she is beyond the fence or in the arena, Katniss makes mental notes of landmarks as she walks and orients her "mental map" based upon these natural landmarks. She always knows where she is because she mentally logs where she has been.

Being aware of the landmarks around you is the most important natural navigation lesson you can learn. Take time to observe the landscape as you walk it. Look for unusual landmarks—a gnarled tree, a creek bed, a rock wall, a patch of flowers. These landmarks will serve as reference points and help you to build a mental map of your surroundings.

Using Nature to Get Home

If you are lost in the woods and your only way home is through self-rescue, there are two landscape features that can help you. Ironically, they are the complete opposite of each other: peaks and valleys.

Get a better view. Climbing to the highest nearby peak can give you several rescue advantages. First, you are more visible to search and rescue teams. Any signals that you deploy can be seen easier from high places versus in dense forest or low terrain. You may also be able to see signs of human activity from high peaks, such as roads, vehicles, or railways. If so, this gives you a certain direction of travel rather than guessing without these visual clues.

Follow water. The opposite of a high peak is a low valley. Chances are if you keep traveling downhill, you will eventually connect with a stream or creek. The general survival rule is

that a stream will lead to a river and a river will lead to people. If you don't know for sure which direction you need to travel and you can't see signs of human activity from a high vantage point, then your best option is to follow water downstream. Eventually, that water will lead you to some sign of human activity. On several instances, Katniss uses the stream as a reference point while traveling through the arena in the Hunger Games. This is an excellent example of building a "mental map" of the area around you.

Using Nature to Find Direction

If you don't have a map or compass to help you head in the right direction, Mother Nature can at least let you know which way is north, south, east, and west.

The Sun: The sun is the easiest way to determine direction. The sun rises in the east and sets in the west. It

YOUR SPONSOR HAS SENT YOU A

SURVIVAL QUICK TIP

When you find water, follow it downstream, meaning walk in the same direction the water is moving. A stream will lead to a river, which will eventually lead to human activity.

Shadow stick method, step 1

Shadow stick method, step 2

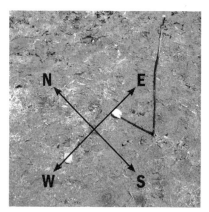

Shadow stick method, step 3

is easy to determine this in the early morning or late evening. Once you know one direction it's easy to determine the other three.

In midday, determining direction from the sun can be a little more difficult—especially when the sun is directly overhead. There is another easy method of finding direction using the sun called the shadow stick method.

Shadow Stick Method for Finding Direction

Step 1: Stake a straight stick (at least 24" [61cm] long) into the ground and place a mark at the very tip of its shadow. Make sure the area where the shadow is cast is flat and free from any other sticks, rocks, or debris.

Step 2: As the sun moves, the shadow will move. Wait about twenty to thirty minutes and make a second mark at the tip of the shadow again. In this example, I've placed a small rock to mark the end of each shadow. The first mark is west and the second mark is east. This is because the sun travels across the sky from east to west.

Step 3: Connect the two marks with a line and complete the compass rose by drawing a perpendicular line through the middle which will represent north and south.

The Stars: What if it's nighttime? The night sky is full of direction

DEFINITION

Compass Rose: A symbol used on compasses and maps to show the orientation of the cardinal directions (north, south, east, west).

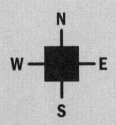

All four directions can be determined by knowing just one direction

indicators—stars. The easiest star to identify is *Polaris*, commonly called the North Star. The most identifiable constellation in the night sky is the Big Dipper and can sometimes be found even on foggy and overcast nights. The outside top corner of the Big Dipper points directly to Polaris. When you've found Polaris, you've found north and you can then determine the other cardinal directions.

Following Natural Landmarks

Whether using a compass, the sun or the stars, it's important to travel using easy-to-see landmarks rather than constantly stopping and checking to make sure you are still traveling in your intended direction. When you decide which direction to travel, face that direction and scan the landscape. Choose an easily distinguished natural landmark, such as a distinctive

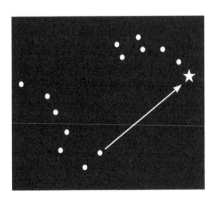

Finding Polaris diagram

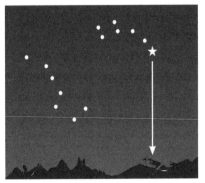

Sample natural landmark using Polaris— now you know the mountain peak is North

A natural landmark, like this large tree, keeps you headed in the same direction.

Strip of bandana as trail marker

tree, mountain peak, or rock formation, to travel toward. Reference this landmark to make sure you are always headed in the same direction. Once you reach your designated landmark, confirm your direction again and then choose a new landmark in the distance. There are countless stories of lost survivors traveling for hours and even days only to find themselves back where they started. Travel smart to avoid this huge waste of time, energy and resources!

SIGNALS, SIGNS, AND RESCUE

Navigating and signaling go hand-in-hand. In the arena, you can use signals as a distraction or to communicate to any allies you may find. In the real-world, signals can save your life. If you become lost or stranded in the wild, ideally rescue crews will also be searching for you by land, water, air,

or all three. In this case, it is critical that you also leave signs (trail markers) of where you've been and the direction you're heading. You'll also want to know a few field-tested rescue signaling techniques.

Leaving Signs of Travel

Remember the story of Hänsel and Gretel? Even though leaving bread crumbs as trail markers didn't work out for them, the concept is still very important. Leaving signs of travel not only allows you to backtrack your path if necessary, but also leaves a trail for rescue teams to follow should they find one of these markers. Katniss uses this tactic when she sprinkles mint leaves around camp to signal to Rue that she had been there. Trail markers can be virtually anything. The important thing is they stand out from the surrounding terrain. These

Rocks arranged in arrow shape indicating direction of travel

Y-stick marker indicating travel to the right

Sticks in arrow shape

Fire triangle diagram

photos show a few examples of trail markers. Some also indicate direction of travel.

Signaling With Fire and Smoke

Fire and smoke signals can prove deadly in the arena. You certainly don't want to give away your location with a careless fire, but if you need to create a distraction or want to throw people off your tracks, a bogus signal fire will work well, as Katniss proves. Fire and smoke are incredibly effective signaling tools.

It's important to build a signal fire in advance of when you need it. In a rescue situation, you want the fire material ready so you can light it as soon as you hear an airplane, boat, or other signs of a rescue party. And you don't want to wait until the rescue crew is in the area to start building the

Building a signal fire, step 1

Building a signal fire, step 2

fire because you may miss them, especially if they aren't headed in your direction. Have the fire ready, but don't burn it until someone will see it. It takes too much energy to keep it fed or continually rebuild it.

At night, the light from fire can be used as a distress signal. A grouping of three fires arranged in the shape of a triangle is a universally understood distress code.

During the day, it's the *smoke* that's important for signaling. The fire material should be dry, protected, and ready to light in a moment's notice. It should also be in the highest place possible and preferably in a clearing that is free from large trees and cliffs that could diffuse or deflect the smoke. Here's how to build a signal fire:

Step 1: Build a log cabin style raised platform to lift your fire off the ground. The platform keeps your fire tinder and pre-prepared kindling from soaking up moisture from the ground. It also helps the fire get a lot of oxygen.

Step 2: Continue to build the walls of the log cabin up from the platform at least 24" (61cm) tall.

Step 3: Fill the interior of the log cabin with the most flammable materials you can find. Dried leaves, dried grass, or cattail down are all perfect options. Then, on top of this tinder material pile on some slightly larger toothpick- to pencil-sized kindling. Make sure everything you use is as dry as possible.

Step 4: In order to create lots of smoke, you must pile a thick layer of

Building a signal fire, step 3

Building a signal fire, step 4

green leafy branches (or pine boughs in winter) on top of the platform. Green, leafy branches create a ton of smoke when burnt. This layer will also protect your dry fire kindling from rain or snow.

You will use the gaps in the log cabin wall to light the dry fire tinder, which will burn incredibly fast. This tinder will quickly catch the more substantial, larger kindling on fire, which will burn the leafy branches or pine boughs. A signal fire like this will only smoke for a few minutes, but that's all the time you'll have or need when signaling for rescue.

If a rescue plane flies overhead before you have a signal fire built, nature does provide a readymade option. Small pine trees and other resinous evergreens make excellent impromptu signal fires. The pinesap, also called resin, contained inside of the pine tree makes it very flammable. Green pine needles smoke like crazy when burnt. Thus, a small pine tree makes a very flammable and smoky pre-built signal fire framework. If you must use this approach, it's best to find a small, lone pine tree (10' [3m] tall or smaller) in an open area so that you don't start a full-blown forest fire.

Signal Mirror

Signal mirrors are included in military survival kits all over the world because they work! The reflection from a mirror can be seen for miles by land, air, or water rescue crews. You can even use the reflection from a bright moon to make a flash at night. A variety of items can be used

Reflective flash on fingers

Flash from a signal mirror

Signal mirror samples: mirror from car visor, rear-view mirror, make-up mirror

Using survival knife blade as signal mirror

as an improvised signal mirror. If it's shiny and reflective, then it will probably work. Your creativity is the limit.

To make your signal most effective, you must aim your mirror at the people you are trying to signal. This requires a little finesse, but the steps are simple.

How to effectively aim a signal mirror:

Step 1: Hold your arm out in front of you and create a "V" with your middle and index fingers.

Step 2: Move your hand so your target (the person, plane or boat you are signaling) is in-between the "V" created by your fingers.

Step 3: Flash the sun's reflection across your fingers. You will be able to see the reflection on your fingers, and this will let you know that the flash is heading out to your target.

Rescue Plane Acknowledgment

How do you know if a rescue plane has seen your signal? Rescue plane pilots are trained to signal back if they see a distress signal. If it's daylight, the pilot should rock the wings of the plane back and forth to confirm that they've spotted you. At nighttime, they should flash the lights as confirmation. If a rescue plane does not reply with one of these confirmation signals or some other kind of direct contact, then you should assume they have not seen your signal and continue your signaling efforts. It's important to watch for and recognize these signals. If you don't understand them, you might decide to keep traveling because you think the plane did not see you.

It's also important to remember that even after a plane has spotted your distress signal, it can still be quite some time before a rescue crew can reach you, so it's important to *stay where you are*. If you received confirmation from a rescue plane, rest assured that a crew is on its way to the location you signaled from.

SUMMARY

If you haven't figured it out yet, survival is a collection of tips, tricks, tools, knowledge, and skills that collectively increase your odds of living through and getting out of a bad situ-

YOUR SPONSOR HAS SENT YOU A

SURVIVAL QUICK TIP

SOS is a universally recognized pattern for distress originating from Morse Code. S is represented by three short dots and O is represented by three longer dashes: ...---... The SOS signal can be sent using sound, but it can also be silently communicated with a flashlight or signal mirror by three short flashes followed by three longer flashes and then again ending with three short flashes. Continue repeating the SOS signal until you receive a response.

ation. The key to surviving the unexpected is preparing in advance for the "what ifs" in life. This involves training your mind with knowledge and survival skills. It also involves keeping a supply of basic survival tools on hand just in case. Packing a survival kit when traveling or venturing into the wilderness is *always* a good idea. Look at it as your own little Cornucopia filled with the survival items that you like and want. Let's explore this concept further in the next chapter.

NINE

RAIDING THE CORNUCOPIA: BUILDING YOUR SURVIVAL KIT

IN THE ARENA, the Cornucopia houses an incredible stash of survival supplies. From weapons and food to tools and gear, it has everything one might need to survive (and thrive) in the wild arena for an extended period of time. It's basically a *huge* survival kit. I would like to take a "shopping" trip to the Cornucopia and stock up on some gear for my own personal kit. And I wonder what Katniss's kit would like if she had the opportunity to build a survival kit from the items in the Cornucopia? Or Gale, what would he choose?

Building a survival kit is at the core of survival training and preparedness. Sourcing survival tools from nature can be difficult, time-consuming and labor intensive. Having a survival kit with a few key items on hand can drastically impact the outcome of a real-life survival scenario. I am a huge fan of carrying some kind of a survival kit (even if it's really small) on you at all times. "Survival kit" can mean a lot of different things to a lot of different people. Here's how I define the term.

Survival Kit: A specialized pre-prepared kit varying in size and shape that contains a variety of items and tools with the sole purpose of sustaining one's life in the event of a life-threatening situation.

With this definition in mind, and based on what we've learned from Katniss's survival mentality, let's explore what you might pack in your own personal survival kit.

CONTAINERS FOR SURVIVAL KITS

Survival kits come in all shapes and sizes. From metal candy tin kits to full-size backpacks, there is no right or wrong size.

A canoeing "dry-sack" makes a wonderful survival kit container. Not only is it waterproof, but it can also be used as a container to carry water.

Survival kit packed in metal candy tin

Willow Haven mini survival necklace kit

I have all kinds of survival kits. I have a disaster survival kit, called a Bug Out Bag, that we will discuss later. I also keep a small survival kit in the glove box of my Ford Bronco. I have a mini kit that I take hiking and fishing. I have a separate survival kit that I take on vacations and even one that I've customized to fit in the hollow stock of my survival shotgun.

Large backpack survival kit

I do prefer for all of my survival kits to be somewhat waterproof. This can be accomplished by wrapping electrical tape around the lids or by sealing the contents in a waterproof plastic bag.

Ideally, every survival kit that you make should include items that help meet needs in the following categories:

- Shelter
- Water
- Fire
- Food
- Tools
- First aid
- Navigation and signaling

The size of your kit will be a big determining factor in what items or what types of items will fit. Let's explore some options.

Two "dry-sacks," one packed with supplies and the other used as water container

SHELTER

A military-style poncho is an excellent shelter solution for a compact survival kit. Not only can it be used as

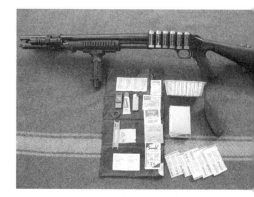

Survival kit packed inside hollow stock of survival shotgun

Military style poncho

Poncho tent

Poncho ridge line lean-to

Poncho diagonal lean-to

a rain poncho, but it can also be set up in many different canopy shelter configurations. Military-style ponchos have metal grommets in each corner that can be used for tie-down points. Many different lightweight tarps also make great impromptu shelters.

An even more compact, lightweight shelter solution is a mylar reflective emergency blanket. These "space blankets" can reflect up to 80 percent of your body heat in a cold-weather environment. They weigh only a few ounces and are about the size of a deck of playing cards when folded. With a little creativity, these blankets can be used as a poncho, a shelter canopy, a waterproof gear cover, a signal flag, or even stripped and used as trail markers.

Survival blanket poncho wrap

Wrapped in survival emergency blanket

Waterproof gear cover

Makeshift lean-to shelter

WATER

Water is vital in a survival situation, but there are three water-related considerations:

1. Containers
2. Collection
3. Purifying

Water Containers

If your kit is large enough, it's smart to pack fresh drinking water in a metal water bottle (I prefer stainless steel). After your packed water is used, you can collect water from natural sources and boil it in the metal bottle to purify it. If you don't pack a water bottle, then you will need to include some kind of container that will allow you to collect water from the wild. I've used all kinds of containers in smaller kits. Some great options are plastic bags and foldable

YOUR SPONSOR HAS SENT YOU A

SURVIVAL QUICK TIP

Survival blankets don't come with tie-down points such as grommets. This can make them tricky to tie down when using them for shelters or gear covers. A quick tip is to put a small rock in the corner and tie your rope around this rock. This creates a very solid tie-down point that will not tear the blanket.

Rock in corner of survival blanket for tie-down point

aluminum containers. Again, water can be boiled for purification in metal aluminum containers.

For very compact survival kits, a great water container option is a non-lubricated latex condom. These are very small and very lightweight yet can hold up to one liter of water. They are amazing little containers.

Many outdoor water bottle companies also make collapsible water containers. These are plastic, bag-like containers that expand to hold a lot of water, yet fold up very small and weigh very little when empty. They are perfect for survival kits. One of my favorites is the Jolly Tank from www.RealitySurvival.com. It can hold up to two gallons of water and is very durable. I also own collapsible bottles by Platypus and Nalgene that I like very much.

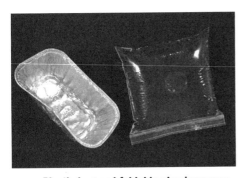

Plastic bag and foldable aluminum pan

Condom with 1 liter of water

Jolly Tank

Platypus and Nalgene collapsible bottles

Aquamira water purification tablets

Purifying

If you are packing a plastic container, you will need a way to purify the water that you collect. Boiling is not a viable option with plastic containers. Katniss has a plastic half-gallon water bottle in her orange pack. She also had liquid iodine, which she uses to purify water. I prefer solid water purification tablets. They are easy to use and very effective against protozoan cysts, bacteria, and viruses. Two brands I would recommend are Katadyn and Aquamira. Simply follow the instructions on your brand of choice. It's important to remember that you must have clear water for chemical purification to take effect. Murky, cloudy, or muddy water drastically affects the efficacy of chemical purifiers, so prefilter your water through a bandana, sock, or shirt to remove as much sediment as possible.

Note: Don't forget to slosh some treated water around the threads of your bottle cap where nasty microbes might be lurking.

FIRE

Without other water purification options, you will need fire in order to boil and purify water. You may also need fire to regulate your core body temperature in cold weather environments. As we've discussed in previous chapters, fire can also signal for

Lighters, ferro rods, and fire tinder

Survival kit food options

Food-related items

rescue, cook food, and help to make containers and tools. It is an essential element in a survival situation. Pack fire-starting tools in every survival kit you make. You need an ignition device, such as a cigarette lighter or ferro rod, and some waterproof fire tinder, such as PET balls, WetFire, or Mini Inferno disks.

FOOD

There are two approaches to food in survival kits. You can use one or the other, or combine the two.

Open-and-Eat Foods

An obvious option is to pack actual food in your kit. The best foods to pack meet two requirements:

1. long shelf lives (for extended storage)
2. can be eaten as is, with no cooking or preparation (open-and-eat foods)

Power bars, protein bars, military MREs (Meals Ready to Eat), beef jerky, trail mix, and soft tuna packets are all great survival food options that meet both requirements. Some other good food-related items include salt, pepper, spices, bouillon cubes, sugar packets, drink mixes, and hard candy.

Hunting and Gathering Tools

If you've read the other chapters in this book, you now know how to

Small survival fishing kit

#2 picture-hanging wire

Cooking wild greens in aluminum foil pan

Fish wrapped in aluminum foil and baked in hot coals

find, catch, gather, and prepare a variety of wild foods. Because of that knowledge, you may also choose to pack items that can help you hunt and gather your own food should that be necessary.

Fishing Kit: A small fishing kit is always at the top of my survival kit list. I include a small fishing kit in *every* survival kit I build—no matter the size. My fishing kit is a combination of various hooks, some fishing line, a few sinkers, a bobber, and maybe a piece of artificial bait, though most fish prefer the real thing.

Snare Wire: In addition, a small coil of snare wire could come in very handy for setting twitch-up snares like those used by Katniss and Gale. I've found that #2 picture-hanging wire, available at almost every hardware store, is perfect for premade

Variety of Metal Pots

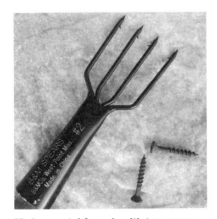

Modern metal frog gig with two screws

Gig mounted to pole and in action

wire snares. You may not have a wire cutter with you when you need to set a snare, so cut your wire in advance. Approximately 18" (46cm) of wire is enough for one small game trap.

Field Guide: In larger kits, a small wild edible field guide is a worthy addition for anyone who is not completely comfortable with their wild plant edible identification skills. The guide I use and recommend is *A Field Guide to Edible Wild Plants: Eastern and Central North America* by Lee Allen Peterson.

Metal Cook Pot: Having a small metal cook pot for preparing meals is a huge bonus and should be considered as an addition to any kit. At a minimum, pack a few feet of aluminum foil, which can be fashioned into temporary cooking, baking, or steaming containers.

I love the stainless steel mug by GSI Outdoors. It is great for cooking 1-cup meals and is virtually indestructible. It also nests perfectly on the bottom of my stainless steel Nalgene water bottle and the 40 oz. stainless Klean Kanteen. I use it for making tea, boiling water, rehydrating meals, and even making 1-cup wild stews. It's a great piece of kit that I highly recommend.

Small Game Gig: In some of my larger survival kits I also pack a modern fish/frog gig. This metal gig is the perfect hunting tool for quick and easy meals. Most gigs come predrilled with holes for screws or nails. Pack a couple small nails or screws with the gig and use them to secure the gig to the end of a branch or limb.

TOOLS

This category can encompass a huge variety of items. The two most important tools in any kit are a cutting tool and a light source. Both are nearly indispensable survival kit items.

Variety of survival kit cutting tools

Cutting Tools

Chapter five discusses the importance of a survival knife, and its essential features, in great detail. I carry one with me at all times and suggest you do the same. Even though you may plan on carrying a fixed-blade survival knife, I still suggest packing a backup cutting tool in any survival kit you build. Your options are limited only to your creativity. In mini kits, I've used X-Acto blades, razor blades, and mini folding knives. In most of my survival kits I simply include a decent-quality folding knife or smaller fixed blade knife.

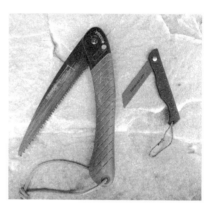

Bahco folding saw (left) and small mini-kit saw (right)

If I have space, I include a saw in some of my survival kits. A nice-quality folding saw can buzz through 3"–4" (8–10cm) thick limbs and saplings in no time at all, making it a worthy addition to any survival kit.

Photon brand LED mini light

Lighting Tools

You have just about as many options with light sources as you do knives. I'm a huge fan of the mini LED keychain lights. They are very small and lightweight. The Photon brand that I use has a crush-proof bulb and the light it produces is visible for more than one mile. Maglite is another brand that makes an excellent mini keychain-size flashlight. These are waterproof and include an extra bulb in the handle.

Mini keychain Maglite

If space allows, a hands-free headlamp is my first choice for a light source. Headlamps provide ample light for normal tasks, such as setting up camp, preparing meals, and traveling. They are lightweight, compact, bright, and long-lasting, and best of all leave your hands free.

Cordage

As you've already discovered, sourcing usable cordage from nature can be difficult and time-consuming. Always pack cordage in your survival kits. I like three kinds of cordage: 550 parachute cord, bank line, and dental floss.

Black Diamond Ion ultralight headlamp

550 parachute cord: Also called "paracord," 550 parachute cord was originally designed as the lines that connected paratroopers to their parachutes. The number 550 indicates that one single strand of parachute cord will hold 550 pounds. This stuff

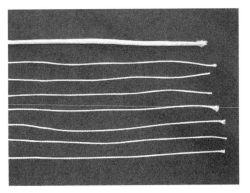

Paracord separated into seven inner strands and nylon sheath

is *very* strong. I love 550 paracord because it consists of a woven nylon outer sheath that contains seven inner nylon strands.

The tensile strength of each inner strand is a surprising 35 pounds. Thus, if you have 10' (3m) of 550 paracord then you actually have 80' (24m) (the outer sheath plus seven inner strands) of usable survival cordage. This is why paracord survival bracelets are so popular amongst survival enthusiasts. Wearing this type of bracelet ensures you always have many feet of usable cordage with you, and it's conveniently kept around your wrist. If you need cordage, you can unravel the bracelet and use it for shelter lashings, bow drill string, fishing line, or snare sets. Find video instructions for making your own paracord survival bracelet at http://www.willowhavenoutdoor.com/paracord-survival-bracelet.

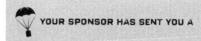

Bank Line: Bank line (also known as trot line) is a nylon twine sold in the fishing section of most outdoor retailers. This style of cordage comes in various weights and strengths. Typically, a length of bank line is fitted with a hook and bait on one end and then tied to a tree or stake on the bank of a pond, river, or stream. The baited end is then thrown into the water and left to fish passively while you do other chores. However, this nylon

Paracord survival bracelet

550 Parachute cord, Bank Line and dental floss

twine can be used for countless other projects besides fishing. I've used bank line for lashing shelters, setting snares, and even as bow and arrow and bow drill strings. It is very strong, durable and lightweight.

Dental Floss: I include a spool of dental floss in almost every survival kit I build. It is truly an amazing cordage. Some spools contain up to 55 yards (50m) of floss and weigh almost nothing! Waxed dental floss can also have a tensile strength up to 20 pounds. That's incredible. It makes excellent cordage for repairing clothing or gear. It also excels as fishing line and small game snare sets. Note: Be sure to buy the plain *non-scented* floss. Strong scents like mint or cinnamon can scare away fish and small game.

FIRST AID

The size of your first aid category really depends on the size of your survival kit. At a minimum, most kits should contain a variety of adhesive bandages, a few gauze pads, some duct tape, and some antiseptic wipes packed in a resealable plastic bag. Adventure Medical Products manufactures an awesome line of first aid kits in a variety of sizes. These are excellent options for larger survival kits.

Below is a detailed list of first aid items you may want to consider including in your own survival kit.

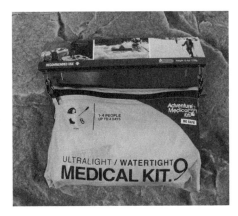

1–4 person Adventure Medical kit

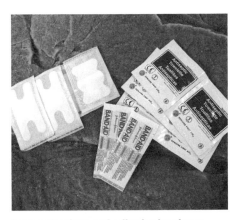

Antiseptic wipes and adhesive bandages

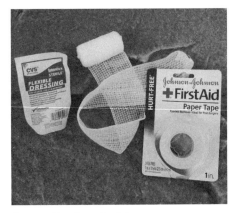

Gauze roll and medical tape

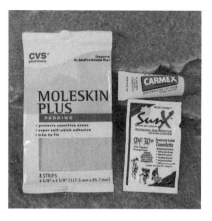

Moleskin, sunscreen towelettes and lip balm

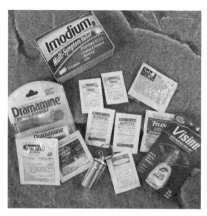

Variety of first aid medicines

Cut and Wound Items

- Antiseptic wipes
- Adhesive bandages—1" × 3" (3cm × 8cm)
- Adhesive bandages—knuckle and elbow
- Adhesive wound closure strips
- Sterile gauze pads (3" × 3") (8cm × 8cm)
- Sterile gauze roll bandage (2" × 6') (5cm × 183cm)
- Medical tape (1" × 30') (3cm × 30m)

Blister/Rash/Burn Treatments

- Moleskin patches (4" × 5") (10cm × 13cm)
- Sunscreen: small tube or towelettes
- Lip balm

Support

- Elastic wrap bandage (3" [8cm] width for wrapping sprained and or strained joints): 6' (183cm)

Medicines/Ointments/Washes

- Antibiotic ointment
- Alcohol swabs
- Ibuprofen pills: reduce fever and treat pain or inflammation
- Antihistamine pills: reduce cold and allergy symptoms
- Acetaminophen pills: reduce fever and treat general aches and pains
- Aspirin pills: reduce fever and treat pain and inflammation
- Antidiarrheal medicine
- Antiemetic (Dramamine): for motion sickness

YOUR SPONSOR HAS SENT YOU A

SURVIVAL QUICK TIP

Rubber gloves are a multi-functional item that can also be used as water containers or to keep items, such as fire tinder, dry.

Rubber gloves, tweezers and safety pins

- Daily prescriptions
- Allergy medicines/emergency allergic reaction medicines
- Asthma inhalers
- Medical instruments (syringes, blood sugar testers, etc).
- Special medications for infants and children
- Visine eye wash

General First Aid Items
- Rubber gloves
- Tweezers: for splinters and ticks

- Safety pins: quantity of five in a variety of sizes
- Insect repellent
- Emergency survival blanket: reflect body heat to prevent hypothermia
- Backup pair of glasses
- Small mirror

NAVIGATION AND SIGNALING
The first-aid/signal mirror is the perfect transition into this survival kit category. There are two options for rescue in a survival scenario:

Two survival-style pack rescue mirrors

Button compass in candy tin survival kit

1. You are found by a rescue crew: air, land, or sea
2. You have to find your own way back to civilization—called self-rescue

Navigation and signaling tools are important for both of these options and, oftentimes, rescue is a combination of many efforts.

Navigation

The obvious navigation tool to include in your survival kit is a compass. Compasses come in all shapes and sizes to fit nearly any sized kit you have in mind. As we discussed earlier in this book, a compass is your sure-fire way to find direction and travel in a straight line.

A topographical map of the surrounding area is also a great addition to any survival kit. For example, if you are taking a three-day hiking trip, be sure to pack a map of the local area just in case you get lost. You may be able to triangulate your location by cross-referencing visible landmarks and ones diagramed on the map (see chapter eight for more details).

Survival Signaling Tools

We've mentioned the use of fire and mirrors as signaling tools. In addition to these, I also suggest packing a small whistle. The brand I use is Fox 40 from www.fox40world.com. It is

YOUR SPONSOR HAS SENT YOU A

SURVIVAL QUICK TIP

Mirrors have many survival uses: first aid, hygiene, and signaling. If you are traveling alone, a mirror is especially useful if you need to self-treat any type of injury to your eyes, face, head, or back. A mirror is also a proven signaling tool. You can purchase signal mirrors specifically designed to help signal rescue planes, vehicles, or teams. These mirrors have a small "sighting hole" in the middle that helps you aim directly at your target. See chapter eight for specific instruction on how to signal with a mirror.

made from a durable polycarbonate that is waterproof and rustproof. It has no moving parts to jam or freeze

Zipper-pull compass on pouch-style survival kit

and can even be blown under water. The 120 dB blast travels for miles.

Signal whistles are far more effective than using your own voice. The whistle blast is *much* louder and travels *much* farther than any sounds you can make by screaming. It also takes far less energy to blow a whistle than to scream.

YOUR PERSONAL TOUCH

At the end of the day, you can put anything you want in a survival kit—it's *your* kit. Chapter one explains the importance of your survival mentality. If you give up mentally, your body will follow suit. Sometimes, in desperate circumstances, a personal item, such as a family photo, a favorite Bible verse, or a picture of a loved one, can give you the mental motivation you need to keep up the good fight and not give up. For this reason, I always include an inspirational item

in every kit I build. I challenge you to do the same with the kits you build. It doesn't take much to remind you that there is too much at stake to give up.

THE CAPITOL IS COMING— BUG OUT!

We live in a crazy world—sometimes I think it's almost as crazy as Panem. Disasters, both natural and man-made, strike when we least expect them and can have devastating consequences— even displacing people from the safety of their homes. The citizens of District 12 experience this first hand when the Capitol invades and forces survivors into the surrounding woods to survive with whatever they could carry with them.

Real-life disasters, such as wind storms, wildfires, tornados, hurricanes, and earthquakes, can cause chaos in the days, weeks, and sometimes months that follow. Electricity

Traditional base plate compass and pin-on ball compass

Variety of survival whistles

The Bug Out Bag

and water service is often cut off to entire cities and regions for at least a short period of time. Oftentimes, these outages will result in food, water, and fuel shortages. Hospitals, police officers, firefighters, and other first responders are overwhelmed with an extraordinary number of disaster victims.

Having a 72-hour disaster survival kit (also called a Bug Out Bag) and some other long-term survival preparations in place is an excellent idea. A Bug Out Bag is basically a large backpack-style survival kit stocked with everything you might need for three days of independent survival. This includes shelter, fire, water, food, tools, clothing, and several other supply categories. Your Bug

Out Bag is the one thing you don't want to forget on your way out the front door in the event of a sudden and unexpected evacuation. There are a lot of great resources available to help you build a Bug Out Bag. Find them in the resources section at the end of this book.

Even if you aren't forced from the safety of your home, it's smart to have a few days' (weeks', even months') worth of fresh water, food, and basic survival necessities on hand should a disaster leave your area without running water, electricity, or access to grocery, fuel, or medical facilities. When one or more of your critical supply chains is interrupted, you'll be glad you've got a small stockpile to depend on until life gets back to normal.

KNOWLEDGE WEIGHS NOTHING

In many instances, skill and knowledge can take the place of pricey and bulky survival gear. Our primitive ancestors used many of the skills outlined in this book for thousands of years to meet their basic survival needs. If you practice these wilderness survival skills, they will sustain you as well. No skill worth having is mastered without trial, error, failure, dedication, and practice. Once you master a skill, it will stay with you forever. You are a survivor!

I will conclude this chapter and book with a poem that I wrote titled "The Survivalist Creedo:"

The Survivalist Creedo

I do not choose to be a victim
Of the circumstances around me.
I seek self-reliance, not dependence.
I do not wish to be looked after,
But rather to be a resource for others.
I am able to provide basic needs
With knowledge and natural tools.
Sometimes I fail, but more often succeed.
Regardless of the outcome, I never give up.
My mind is my most valuable resource.
I understand that Mother Nature is not my mother,
But will still provide me with my basic needs;
Water, Food, Fire & Shelter.
I prefer a landscape view
Over the view across my desk.
I yearn to be outdoors—learning, exploring, and connecting.
I sleep more peacefully under the stars,
Than under a roof.
I am self-sufficient.
I see value in primitive survival skills.
Fire is one of my prized accomplishments,
And my knife is my loyal companion.
I practice my skills and train my body,
For the day when I might be tested.
With everything to lose,
And everything to gain,
Luck has no place in my destiny.
With God's help,
I have made the preparations necessary to get me through.
I am a Survivalist.

SURVIVAL KIT RESOURCES

THIS SECTION INCLUDES resources for finding and using the equipment and materials discussed in this book. It also includes at-home exercises that you can follow to hone your survival skills. When an exercise includes fire, have a large bucket of water and/ or fire extinguisher on hand (even if you're only lighting tinder). If you are under the age of eighteen, don't attempt the fire-related exercises unless you have an adult with you. Always thoroughly extinguish a fire after you are finished using it.

SHELTER

Adventure Medical Kits heat sheet
- www.adventuremedicalkits. com
- willowhavenoutdoor.com

Military grommeted poncho
- Army/Navy surplus stores
- www.mainemilitary.com

Lightweight Back-Packing Tent
- local outdoor retailers
- www.campmor.com

All-weather super emergency blanket
- willowhavenoutdoor.com

At-Home Exercises
- Learn how to tie the following knots by memory: taut-line hitch, double half hitch, and siberian hitch. I use these knots with every shelter I build. Find an instructional video on how to tie these knots at willowhavenoutdoor.com.
- Practice setting up an emergency shelter using a poncho, tarp, trash bag, or emergency blanket.

WATER

Stainless steel water bottles
- nalgene.com
- www.kleankanteen.com
- www.rei.com
- willowhavenoutdoor.com

Collapsible water bottles
- nalgene.com
- www.kleankanteen.com
- www.rei.com
- willowhavenoutdoor.com
- www.realitysurvival.com

Water purification systems, tablets and information
- water.epa.gov/drink/emer-prep/emergencydisinfection. cfm
- www.aquamira.com
- www.katadyn.com/usen
- www.sawyer.com/water.html

At-Home Exercises
- Use a tarp, poncho or sheet of plastic to build a rain catch.

- Practice bringing water to a boil in a metal container over a fire.
- Practice bringing water to a boil using the rock-boiling method in chapter three.
- Practice collecting water from wild grapevines as discussed in chapter three.

FIRE

Ferro rods/fire starters
- www.kodiakfirestarters.com/demonstration/
- www.lightmyfire.com
- willowhavenoutdoor.com
- www.thepathfinderschoolllc.com
- www.ultimatesurvival.com/ust_website/root/fire_starting.html

Do-it-yourself fire tinder
- willowhavenoutdoor.com/general-survival/the-best-fire-starter-money-cant-buy-pet-balls-dryer-lint-fire-starter

At-Home Exercises
- Practice building a fire large enough to cook a meal and boil water. Do this in all seasons and after it rains. Practice building a fire platform to protect your fire from the wet ground or snow.

- Practice collecting and igniting naturally found fire tinder, such as dry grasses, cattail down, and birch bark. Mix your petroleum jelly or lip balm with natural found tinder to see how it can be used as a flame extender. (Thoroughly clean the petroleum jelly from your hands before you light the tinder.)
- Practice lighting tinder by concentrating sun rays with a magnifying glass, glass bottle, or clear bag filled with water.
- Build a bow drill set and practice creating an ember with it.

FOOD

Survival food items and Military MREs (Meals Ready to Eat)
- www.mre-meals.net/index.php
- www.nitro-pak.com
- wisefoodstorage.com
- www.thereadystore.com
- local grocery markets

Field Guide to Edible Wild Plants: Eastern and Central North America by Lee Allen Peterson
- local bookstores
- online booksellers
- willowhavenoutdoor.com

At-Home Exercises

- Try to find as many of the wild edible plants mentioned in chapter six growing wild in you area as possible. Make yourself very familiar with these plants. Download the full-color reference sheets at www.livingreadyonline.com/hungergamesedibles.
- Practice your tracking and stalking skills. Look for game trails and animal scat. Practice being still and silent in the woods.

TOOLS

Snare wire/survival traps

- www.thompsonsnares.com
- willowhavenoutdoor.com
- www.bepreparedtosurvive.com
- local hardware store

Survival fishing kits

- www.thepathfinderschoolllc.com
- www.bepreparedtosurvive.com
- local fishing and outdoor retailers

Frog gigs

- www.eagleclaw.com
- willowhavenoutdoor.com
- www.bnmpoles.com

Knives and cutting tools

- www.hedgehogleatherworks.com
- willowhavenoutdoor.com
- kosterknives.com
- www.bigrockforge.com

Paracord and Paracord Products

- www.combatparacord.com
- willowhavenoutdoor.com
- www.bucklerunner.com

Bank line

- local outdoor retailer—fishing section
- willowhavenoutdoor.com
- www.thepathfinderschoolllc.com

At-Home Exercises

- Practice carving feather sticks with your survival knife (with adult supervision if you're under eighteen).
- Gather grapevine, pine root, inner tree bark, and plant fiber and practice reverse-wrapping them to create cordage.

LIGHTING PRODUCTS

- willowhavenoutdoor.com
- www.campmor.com
- www.photonlight.com
- local outdoor retailers

FIRST AID KITS AND PRODUCTS

Premade first aid kits
- www.adventuremedicalkits. com
- www.nitro-pak.com
- www.medcallassist.com

Miscellaneous first aid supplies
- local pharmacy

NAVIGATION AND SIGNALING

Survival signal mirrors
- willowhavenoutdoor.com
- www.adventuremedicalkits. com
- www.campingsurvival.com

Survival whistles
- www.campingsurvival.com
- www.fox40world.com

Compasses, orienteering skills, and natural navigation
- www.silvacompass.com
- www.naturalnavigator.com
- www.us.orienteering.org/ content/orienteering-skills

At-Home Exercises
- Use a compass in coordination with a paper map to reach a destination.
- Practice building a signal fire as described in chapter eight.

Note how much foliage is needed to make a significant amount of smoke.
- Use the shadow stick method (described in chapter eight) to determine the cardinal directions. Then use a compass to see how accurate your results are.
- On a clear night, practice finding Polaris, the north star.
- Practice signaling a friend using a mirror.
- Lead a friend through the woods using trail markers, such as bandanas, rocks, or sticks (see chapter eight). Then reverse roles and follow your friend's trail markers through the woods.

DISASTER PREPAREDNESS

General information
- www.ready.gov
- www.redcross.org
- www.cdc.gov
- willowhavenoutdoor.com

How to Build a Bug Out Bag
- www.ready.gov
- Book: *Build the Perfect Bug Out Bag* by Creek Stewart (local bookstores, online booksellers, willowhavenoutdoor.com)

Web resources for survival articles, information and instruction

- willowhavenoutdoor.com
- www.realitysurvival.com
- thesurvivalmom.com
- apartmentprepper.com
- saltnprepper.com
- www.prepperwebsite.com
- foodstorageandsurvival.com
- www.thepreparednessreview.com

Survival and disaster preparedness schools, classes and training

- American Red Cross, www.redcross.org
- Willow Haven Outdoor, Indiana, willowhavenoutdoor.com
- The Pathfinder School, LLC, Ohio, www.thepathfinder-schoolllc.com

INDEX

ABOUT THE AUTHOR

Creek Stewart specializes in disaster pre-paredness and has consulted with individu-als, corporations, nonprofits, and govern-ment agencies all over the United States about a myriad of preparedness-related sub-jects, projects, and initiatives.

A lifelong student of survival, pre-paredness and self-reliance, Creek Stewart wrote his first survival manual at the age of twenty-one. Soon thereafter, Creek began teaching survival and primitive skills courses on his family farm in Southern Indiana.

He now owns Willow Haven Outdoor, a leading survival and preparedness training facility that is 10,000 sq. ft. in size and situated on twenty-one beauti-ful acres in central Indiana. For information about survival clinics and training courses, visit www.willowhavenoutdoor.com.

Creek is an Eagle Scout and graduate of Butler University in Indianapolis.

DEDICATION

I dedicate this book to Omaha Hoyt. Good luck on your survival journey to London. For more information visit willowhavenoutdoor.com.

Published by Living Ready, an imprint of F+W Media, Inc., 700 East State St., Iola, WI 54990. (800) 289-0963. First Edition.

Other fine Living Ready books are available from your local bookstore and online suppliers. Visit our website at www.livingreadyonline.com.

17   16   15   14   13   5   4   3   2   1

ISBN 978-1-4403-2855-8

Distributed in Canada by Fraser Direct
100 Armstrong Avenue, Georgetown, Ontario, Canada L7G 5S4
Tel: (905) 877-4411

Distributed in the U.K. and Europe by F&W Media International, LTD
Brunel House, Forde Close, Newton Abbot, TQ12 4PU, UK
Tel: (+44) 1626 323200, Fax: (+44) 1626 323319
E-mail: enquiries@fwmedia.com

Distributed in Australia by Capricorn Link
P.O. Box 704, S. Windsor NSW, 2756 Australia
Tel: (02) 4560-1600
Fax: (02) 4577-5288
E-mail: books@capricornlink.com.au

Edited by Jacqueline Musser
Designed by Clare Finney
Production Coordinated by Debbie Thomas

MORE BOOKS ON SURVIVAL AND PREPAREDNESS

Build The Perfect Bug Out Bag
By Creek Stewart

Survive! The Disaster, Crisis and Emergency Handbook
by Jerry Ahern

Stay Alive!
by John D. McCann

AVAILABLE ONLINE AND IN BOOKSTORES EVERYWHERE!

To get started join our mailing list at www.livingreadyonline.com.

Become a fan of our Facebook page:
facebook.com/LivingReady